D0168363

Work Addiction
Hidden Legacies Of Adult Children

Bryan E. Robinson, Ph.D.

Health Communications, Inc.
Deerfield Beach, Florida

Bryan E. Robinson, Ph.D.
Charlotte, North Carolina

Library of Congress Cataloging-in-Publication Data

Robinson, Bryan E.
    Work addiction : hidden legacies of adult children / by
Bryan E. Robinson.
       p.   cm.
    Bibliography: p.
    ISBN 1-55874-023-6
    1. Workaholism.   I. Title.
RC569.5W67R63   1989   88-32634
616.85'227—dc19   CIP

Publisher: Health Communications, Inc.
          3201 S.W. 15th Street
          Deerfield Beach, Florida 33442

Dedication

To my most important teachers:

To Jamey McCullers for showing me the difference between lettuce and cabbage, how to tie a necktie and especially for showing me the light at the end of the tunnel.

To Lauren Stayer for reminding me how important I am.

Contents

Introduction

1. All About Me: Confessions Of A Precocious
   Over Worker (POW) 1
2. What Is Work Addiction Syndrome? 23
3. Common Characteristics Of Work Addicts 39
4. Work Addicts Speak Out 65
5. How CoAs Become Work Addicts: The Cycle
   Of Addiction 87
6. Children Of Work Addicts: Breaking The
   Cycle Of Addiction 107
7. Work Addiction In The Workplace 115
8. Steps To Personal Recovery 137
9. References And Further Readings 169

Acknowledgments

Without the cooperation and assistance of many colleagues, friends and family members, this book would not have been possible. I appreciate the steadfast personal and administrative support of Dr. Mary Thomas Burke and Dr. Harold H. Heller. I give special thanks to the following people for their love, support and sharing of themselves in the preparation of this book:

Barbara Armstrong	Lorraine Penninger
Audrey Belk	Jan Phillips
Marion Brennan	Bobbie Rowland
Bettie Dibrell	Ralph Rowland
Linda Hamilton	Doris Schlitt
Sharon Jennings	Ellie Shepherd
Bob Kennedy	Dennis Stabler
Glenda Loftin	John Stayer
Susan Marash-Minnerly	Lauren Stayer
Jamey McCullers	Patty Stayer
Bob Miller	Pauline Tulson
Sue Rosen Patterson	Charles Watrous

Introduction

In March of 1988 I stepped onto the stage, making my acting debut at 43 years of age. The extent of my acting experience had been a butterfly in the third grade. As Head Butterfly, it was my job to flitter around and wake up all the sleepy little flowers. Now 35 years later, with the life of a child of an alcoholic under my belt, I donned my powdered wig and hit the stage again. This time I played John Rugby in Shakespeare's *Merry Wives of Windsor*. I not only debuted my acting abilities but also my new life in recovery from work addiction.

Dramatically speaking it was a small part — only three or four lines in three scenes. But in the drama of life it was my biggest role ever. The experience was a humbling one, to say the least. I played a servant who was beaten, pushed, pulled, kicked and ordered around. I was a "slack" servant at that — someone who always tried to avoid work. No typecasting here. My character was the complete opposite from the true me who was resistant to authority and addicted to work.

Although I was not the "big cheese" as I was accustomed to being, the role symbolized a new turn of events — a life without hurry and without a concrete product to show for my efforts, a life of comfort in an unfamiliar role. I was actually *playing* a role in which I had to separate myself from the character, be spontaneous and flexible, and let go of my stiff and stodgy persona. And I was supposed to be having fun all the while.

My need for control and predictability was challenged as my lines were cut in some places and added in others. Scenes were changed, and I was put in some and deleted from some. One night I thought, "Now, I hope things are finally set." But I had put myself into a world that required fluidity. It was a process where you try things out that might fit and see what works. Gradually, I learned to let go, do as I was told and go with the flow. "Try things," the director would say. "Play with your character."

In rehearsals when I'd miss a cue, I felt devastated. I was harder on myself than the director was. "Relax," she'd say. "Everybody misses a cue once in a while. This is supposed to be fun!"

At first I took my small role too seriously, as I did everything in life. I approached rehearsals like I had always approached my work. I learned that I was the puppeteer of my own puppet and, as such, only I could let loose of the strings. Simultaneously applying everything I learned from the 12 Steps of Al-Anon, I learned another part of who I am and what I can do. I discovered that living is not a series of projects to turn out like an assembly line, and that the process can be meaningful and satisfying. I truly felt whole, as if my life had shifted toward a more complete balance.

During our final bows, I felt sheer exhilaration. I had just accomplished one of the most important roles in life and neither the audience nor the cast knew the significance of this small part in my venture toward self-discovery.

Work addiction, although it is the most accepted and encouraged of all the addictions, is a serious disease that destroys relationships and kills people. Held hostage by their illness, work addicts live in misery and despair amid accolades, slaps on the back, fat paychecks and gold plaques. It is the only disease that draws cheers from onlookers as the work addict dies a slow painful death, both psychologically and physically. Our society needs an overhauling on its views of work, at the personal, human and corporate levels. We must learn to make distinctions between healthy work habits and work abuse. We need to reward healthy work habits and provide employee assistance for workers driven on the job.

This book explores the disease of work addiction against the backdrop of an alcoholic or dysfunctional family upbringing. While many adult children become chemically dependent, develop eating disorders or other forms of compulsive behaviors, a large group uses work as their drug of choice. Many of them fool themselves into believing that they have overcome the family illness when, in fact, it has insinuated itself through abusive work patterns. Switching addictions into work is the most acceptable yet dangerous form of addiction for which little help is available.

The book is also for concerned employers who are interested in optimal work conditions for their employees.

This is a synthesis of my clinical work with children of alcoholics in an outpatient treatment center, my life as a child of an alcoholic and recovering work addict, and my experience in Al-Anon and Adult Children of Alcoholics groups.

My goal is to raise the awareness about the disease of work addiction, distinguish between healthy and addictive work patterns, and provide a plan for recovery.

The case studies are based on real people. All names have been changed to protect the persons' anonymity. In some instances I have used composite examples of several respondents to ensure privacy and confidentiality.

1

All About Me: Confessions Of A Precocious Over Worker (POW)

Flames engulfed our tiny wood-frame house. I was five years old. I remember standing, paralyzed by fear, as the fire roared and swelled. My older sister and I huddled together in terror as neighbors worked frantically to retrieve household belongings from the raging inferno. A gas kitchen stove had exploded, I heard someone say. Minutes before I had witnessed flames leaping up the kitchen wall and my mother's sharp demands for me to hurry for sand as she desperately tried to douse them. And I vaguely remember my mother's moans of horror after head counting her three children and realizing that her 18-month-old daughter was still inside the burning house.

A legend grew from that incident and was told and retold by friends and neighbors for the rest of my childhood. A brave neighbor, so the story goes, rescued the toddler by rushing through the blaze, picking her up from a circle of dancing flames and tossing her to safety over the heads of curious onlookers. My older sister insists that the real truth is less intriguing. She had picked up baby sister and carried her to safety before the fire started burning out of control and she had never really been in any danger at all. In the confusion no one agrees about what really happened that day, but my younger sister suddenly appeared in my mother's arms in fine shape.

The fire continued to rage out of control until our house was burned to the ground. We were left with nothing, except for a few pieces of furniture and the clothes on our backs. No one notified my father of the disaster. He came home as usual that afternoon to find his house in smouldering ruins. He didn't know what had happened to cause the fire or if his family had perished in it. Standing beside him in silence, I didn't know what was going through his mind at that moment. But like all five-year-olds, I figured he was thinking the same thing I was. Looking up at his sad and defeated face from my small stature, I felt inside the way he looked on the outside. Pondering over the charred remains, we wondered and worried about what we would do now.

In many ways that fire symbolized my entire childhood. The volatileness, rage and chaos of the burning house embodied the spirit of its inhabitants. When I recount my early family life, I think of it as unpredictable and torridly raging out of control. You might even say it was hell. I always thought that mine was an unusual childhood — unique enough that it would make a bestseller. After studying chemical dependency and families, working with children of alcoholic parents for years and hearing other childhood stories, mine was not so different from all the rest. In fact, my upbringing was bland by comparison to most.

A Sea Of Denial

I grew up on the edge of a large city in the rural South. The term "alcoholic" was not part of the vernacular of that region. I never even heard the word until I was grown. We had one local drunk, Ed Quick, and even he was never called an alcoholic. The only reason he was a reputed drunk is that he slept wherever he fell each night — in a ditch, in the woods or on someone's doorstep. He was the butt of jokes, as well as the scapegoat for other heavy drinkers, who needed proof that they didn't have a drinking problem because *they* didn't fall down in the streets.

It was the custom that if you drank behind closed doors, your reputation could not be impugned no matter how much you drank, how it affected you or where you fell drunk in your own home. Drinking was part of the custom. It was all around me as I grew up. Nobody thought twice about it and if somebody's drinking got out of hand, you'd simply hear, "He tied one on last night," or "He had one too many." There was community denial about alcoholism as well as family denial. To this day my mother denies that my father was an alcoholic. "He was a drunkard," she contends, despite the fact that when he died, he had cirrhosis of the liver.

After I grew up, I learned that the county in which I lived had the highest rate of alcoholism in my home state which, in turn, had a larger rate of alcoholism than is found among the general population. I was surrounded by alcohol from the day I was born. No wonder drinking and seeing neighbors drunk was so normal to my eyes. No wonder that the denial in the family and community was so strong. We couldn't see the forest for the trees.

It wasn't the drinking per se that caused the turbulence in my childhood. In fact, I have few memories of my father actually consuming alcohol. It was the bizarre behavior that the drinking wrought, the breakdown of healthy communication and the development of childhood survival techniques that, while appearing to work at the time, would ultimately cause me great difficulty in adult life. I hold no memories of the old house that burned — only of those in the rebuilt house after I was five. Little did I know that the next five years of my life would be the worst.

New House, Old Habits

Within two years my hard-working and resourceful father had managed to finance the rebuilding of our house on the same plot of land where it had burned. Ironically, although we had a new house, our home — our family — continued to decay.

It was 1950 and my father worked as a machinist in a plant that manufactured guided missiles. He worked long and hard. My mother stayed home and managed the house. I have no memories of my parents ever smiling at each other, having light-hearted fun or embracing. Through my childhood eyes, the only time they spoke was to complain or disagree, and the only time they touched was to hit or slap. My father started drinking in the open at home until my mother bitterly complained that he should not drink in front of the kids. Perhaps that's why I remember little about his actually putting a bottle to his lips, but have many memories of his drunken episodes.

Weekends Were The Worst

Friday nights were usually movie nights. When I was eight, Daddy, as I called him true to Southern tradition, would take my younger sister and me to the movie theater about three miles from home and leave us there; he promised to be back by a certain time but rarely was. More often than not, it became routine for us to walk out with the manager after seeing the same movie two or three times. Many nights we stood outside the theater as the marquee darkened and the street traffic quieted down in the still night. We never knew whether or not he would remember to come back for us. Underneath the big-screen excitement of James Dean and Marilyn Monroe was a little boy's constant worry that his father had abandoned him.

Sometimes we were able to get rides home with parents of our friends. I always rejected the manager's offers to take us home saying, "Oh, he'll be here after a while. He just got busy." Naturally, I wanted to believe that and above all I didn't want the manager to know the truth: that this man had become so busy drinking, he'd forgotten about his children. Sometimes my sister would cry and, although I wanted to, I had to make her think I was in charge of the situation. I was scared and mad because of the cold and the dark empty streets. How could our father be so thoughtless if he truly loved us? My feelings of abandonment were expressed through anger that camouflaged deeper emotions of hurt and rejection.

Sometimes Daddy would pull up at twelve or one in the morning. Other times strange men (who must have been more sober "drinking buddies") would come for us and say our father had sent them. We were always frightened of these strangers because we didn't know if they were telling the truth or if they would hurt us.

One Friday night Daddy dropped us off and instructed us that he would be back at a certain hour and that we should be standing in a specific spot at that time. As kids, we became fastidious about time and locations because we had to make sure that any mix-ups had not been our mistake in judgment. We waited in the designated spot for hours, but he never came. It was late and dark. Finally a taxi driver pulled up beside us and said that our father had sent him to pick us up. Emotionally and physically exhausted, we reluctantly went with the stranger.

When Daddy never showed, the police would take us home. Riding in the police car embarrassed and scared me because I felt like I had done something wrong, and I didn't want neighbors and friends to see the officers pull up in front of my house. After one or two rides in a squad car, I learned an alternate solution. From then on, I insisted that we walk the three miles home over the protests of my tired little five-year-old sister. I learned quickly that the drudgery and fear of a three-mile hike in the dark was less painful than the humiliation of standing in front of the theater in full view of the other children who had rides or of riding in a police car like a criminal.

Saturdays would be different, we convinced ourselves, because that was the day we always went into town to buy things. Daddy was a generous man and bought us practically anything within reason that we wanted. He usually kept a bottle in the glove compartment of his Chevrolet. After parking the car, he'd always reach for the bottle and take a big gulp before going to the bank or to the five and dime. One day as he put the bottle to his lips, two of my schoolmates passed by. They looked at me and waved, and then looked at my dad with a strange look coming over their faces. I was so ashamed that after that day, I pretended I didn't see my friends when my folks took me to town.

Daddy would end up spending hundreds of dollars on clothes for us. But by the time we would get inside the department stores to try on outfits, he'd be stumbling and slurring his words. The stares from clerks and other shoppers would embarrass me so badly that I wanted to disappear. The expensive clothes were not important anymore, and I just wanted to leave.

To avoid the shame of being seen with my father, I eventually convinced him to set up an expense account for my sisters and me at the best shop in town. From then on I walked downtown after school and did my own shopping without the burden of Saturday morning humiliations. At 10 years of age, this experience made me more independent, and I learned to purchase and coordinate my own outfits when most kids' parents still did that for them.

Sundays in the South were big days for visiting relatives and eating large home-cooked meals. Our favorite place for Sunday lunch was my father's sister's house. She'd make huge platters of fried chicken, heaping bowls of rice and gravy, and mounds of homemade biscuits. As kids, we loved to pop in unannounced and sit down at the table with her, my uncle and our cousins. We always felt welcomed and enjoyed the conversations and the delicious food. After eating, the children had a good time playing while the adults lounged under the shade trees.

Those wonderful lazy Sundays were the best days of the weekend and usually the quietest times because we were with other people who loved us and enjoyed our company. At least, we thought this at the time. Once grown, however, our cousins confided in us that they always resented it when we drove up right at lunchtime and interrupted their family meals. We learned that they were nice to us because they felt sorry for us and had been instructed by their mother to be kind. It was the least a dutiful sister could do for her alcoholic brother. But the truth was that we had been in the way. Hearing that helped us, as adults, to reinterpret those pleasant early images of relatives who loved and cared for us into more realistic ones of relatives who perceived us as burdens and who barely tolerated our unwelcomed presence. As it turned out, our best day of the weekend had been enjoyed at the expense of the happiness of others.

Stuffing My Feelings

I was embarrassed by the way my father behaved and was afraid people wouldn't like me because of it. He seemed to care more for his bottle than he did for us. My sense of self-worth nosedived. If my father couldn't remember to pick me up at the movies, I figured I must not be very important. My natural way to cope with these feelings at a very young age was to emotionally disconnect myself from my family. I became very shy and withdrawn. I felt alone. I thought that others were better than me and that I was no good at all. For years I kept all my feelings bottled up inside and never let anybody know how I felt.

Little did I know that my heart showed through my sad eyes and face. To my teachers at school I was an average and shy little boy from an ordinary family who never made trouble and always wanted to do well to please others.

My third grade teacher once asked me in front of the class, "Bryan, why don't you ever smile?" Although she was a kind teacher and probably had only the best of intentions, I was devastated. I realized that she had detected my hidden secret and that I should smile more often to conceal my feelings. From then on and even into adulthood, my smile became my mask. I began to smile to conceal my real feelings and to offset any suspicions. Sometimes I found myself smiling for no apparent reason — not because I was happy but because I wanted to hide the fact that I was sad.

Taking Control Of The Situation

During the next few years, things got worse at home. To avoid confrontations with my mother, Daddy started hiding beer and liquor bottles. I was always discovering them in closets, cabinets and dresser drawers. One day I found a hidden bottle of whisky in a kitchen cabinet. As a meager attempt to control his drinking, I poured out the alcohol and filled the bottle with apple vinegar which resembled the color of the whisky. "That would stop him once and for all," my 10-year-old mind reasoned. When he took a swig of the vinegar, he grimaced, became enraged and beat me unmercifully. I never tampered with his bottles again.

My father started "working longer hours" — until eight or nine o'clock at night. Eventually, he stopped coming home at all. He would stay out all night and on some weekends he would stay gone the entire weekend. That's when the violence erupted and that's when my memories are sharpest, for that's when I had to take center stage.

My stomach flip-flopped. It always did that when Daddy finally made it home and staggered up the porch steps at a late hour. I quaked in my bed as I heard him fumbling around for his house keys because I knew another sleepless night was about to begin. The lights would come on all over the house. My mother was up, determined to find out what woman he'd been with until three in the morning. My sisters would scurry around too, and true to tradition, the whole house would be in an uproar.

When Daddy became drunk, which he did with increasing frequency, I'd jump out of bed to manage the situation. My parents' words became sharper and louder, and more violent. A vicious cycle developed between them. The more Daddy drank, the more Mother complained and the more she complained, the more he drank. She accused him of seeing other women. He accused her of making his life so miserable that he had no place to come home to. They were so consumed with their own feelings and preoccupations that they didn't stop to consider the children. We were left to survive on our own the best we could in a world we didn't understand. My house became a battleground and we became the spoils of war.

Our home was an arsenal of weapons. A new lamp had a maximum life of 48 hours. Kitchen knives, dishes, frying pans, knick-knacks, mirrors, pictures off the wall, hairbrushes and even furniture were all heaved, thrown, slung and slammed during weekly angry outbursts between my parents. My house was always in disarray. I hid things so that they wouldn't get broken. Sweeping up shattered glass, plastic or debris became a weekly ritual.

My 17-year-old sister had married and left home, and I had become ringmaster of our family circus. To avoid temper flare-ups, I tried to clarify verbal assaults, "Mother didn't really mean it that way." I ended up refereeing verbal bouts that sometimes lasted for hours. "Okay, that's enough, now stop it! Be quiet!" Sometimes my interventions developed into pleading as a last resort, "Please don't call her that." I would beg them to stop and settle their differences quietly. But ultimately, as quarrels turned into physical threats, I stood between my father's threatening fist, defiant stare and bloodshot eyes, and my mother's raised arm. It was like trying to separate two fighting dogs and getting bitten in the scuffle.

When I interfered, they would strike wildly at me or push me away so that they could resume their battle. As small as I was, it was an impossible job to manage, and I had to sidestep their swats at me. Realizing I couldn't prevent the inevitable, I busied myself scurrying around jerking windows and curtains closed to insulate the domestic war from the eyes of curious neighbors and hiding wall hangings and fragile figurines from the coffee table, most of which were already dented or chipped from previous abuse.

I had become the one who ran the show: the protector, the peacemaker, the referee, the judge, the family hero or the general. The seeds of precocious over worker (POW) were being planted. Although I couldn't stop the violence, I could control the scenario so that neighbors would not see, the house would not be destroyed and no one would be killed or sent to the hospital or prison. It was not a role I chose; it was one that I took by default, out of necessity and out of a will to survive.

Eventually, I discovered that my best recourse was to withdraw from my family altogether. From the time I could hold a pencil, I spent hours alone in my room writing mystery stories about characters that I created in my mind. I loved it because these characters would do anything that I wanted them to do. I had full rein over them. Writing not only gave me a sense of control over my unwieldy life, but also provided a sanctuary from all the inexplicable events that surrounded and threatened to engulf me. My pretend stories became plays that I'd make my neighborhood friends act out. I was not only the writer, but also the director. We'd hang up old bedspreads for curtains, and my front porch would be the stage.

In high school I wrote and directed the annual church Christmas play, and even designed the sets and acted in the role of the lead character. I didn't know it at the time, but now I realize that creating characters and directing others on what to say and how to behave gave me immense control and a sense of stability that served as an antidote to the instability of my home life. Paradoxically, these activities were also the origins of an addiction to work that would stalk me into adulthood.

After years of seeing my parents out of control, I began to deplore any situation in which people could not control themselves. I learned very early to *always* be in control. When violence erupted between my parents, I learned to stay poised, ready to intercede to keep them apart, to hide breakable items, and generally to try to keep them from killing each other or one of us, or from destroying the house a second time.

Then, after calm descended on us as it always did in the wee hours of morning, I cleaned up the mess and made everything look as if nothing had happened. A scrupulous eye, however, could discern clues from chipped glass figurines, dented furniture and holes in the wall.

There were many trips to the hospital and the police station, and there were many times the police visited us, sometimes at a concerned neighbor's request. I always hated it when the secret slipped out. As long as nobody knew what was happening, I grew to assent and even preferred putting up with it. In fact, I would rather contend with the violent nights than have anyone find out. Daybreak was always a welcome sight. As morning finally broke and quiet descended over the house, I could breathe a sigh of relief because I knew my family had made it through another night.

From then on, I remember my father drunk. I honed my skills carefully and became expert at assessing his sobriety by the time his feet left the 1958 Chevy and touched ground. It was a look he had about him, his vacant stare and downturned lips. I immediately began preparing the house for what had become the only predictable thing in my young life — turmoil. For the next 15 minutes I would remove breakable objects, close windows and curtains, hide anything that could cause

harm, and try to smooth tense conversations. I thought
I was successful in concealing our family secret from
neighbors. I thought that no one knew. But as I grew
older, I discovered that everybody did.

We walked on eggshells and had to be careful what we
said and how we said it, for through my father's
intoxicated eyes, the simplest comment could be misin-
terpreted and could ignite his temper. We had to be
careful laughing or giggling so that he wouldn't think we
were laughing at or making fun of him. Any subtle
movement of the hand, raised eyebrow or smiling face
took on exaggerated meaning in my father's mind.
Ultimately, it did not matter what we said or did because
it was through violence that he expressed his inner
helplessness and frustration.

One night in particular he had been drinking heavily.
I was sleeping with and caring for my baby sister who
was still recuperating from a tonsillectomy. A roaring
fire in our living room fireplace warded off a bitter cold
winter's night. From the bedroom where I slept with
my ailing sister, I heard the sounds of angry, muted
voices. I put my arm around her as a sign that
everything would be okay. Suddenly, the door was
flung open and the lights came on. Deafening sounds
of a drunken rampage broke the silence of the room.
Daddy picked up an old lantern that I had found in an
abandoned house and slung it at us. It hit my sister in
the head. As she began to cry, he jerked the telephone
cord out of the wall, marched into the living room and
flung the phone into the fire. My mother yelled at him
and they pushed each other.

But my attention was focused on the melting telephone. That sight so terrified me that I felt my lifeline to
the world had been severed. To me that act symbolized
a disconnection from a world that I longed to become a
part of and a loss of hope of ever escaping from the
home that had become my prison.

At the time I had to suppress my own feelings and
think only of my sister. As my parents continued

screaming and hitting each other, I bundled her up and drove illegally (I was only 15 years old) five miles to my older sister's house. I had been given an old 1950 Dodge with no heater in anticipation of reaching my sixteenth birthday and getting my driver's license. Although we could see our breath in the cold, our emotions numbed us from the freezing weather. We drove in silence, only broken by my sister's whimpers. We must have looked like two waifs suddenly appearing in the cold on Big Sister's doorstep in the middle of her dinner party. Through tears of fear, anger and exasperation, I related what had happened. I'll never forget feeling her secure arms around me, the warmth of her house and the calm that suddenly embraced us.

There were other minor attempts to physically escape our family's alcoholism. One day little sister packed her belongings in a cigar box and ran away from home. She returned within an hour because she didn't know where else to go. Although that action drew chuckles from my parents, it was a little girl's futile cry for help. Eventually, it was clear that we could not escape our fate. So we acquiesced to it. My writing took on more importance as my refuge, and I even had a cheap typewriter on which to pound out my thoughts and feelings. Another part of me no longer cared what happened, and there were even times when I wished my father were dead.

Dr. Jekyll And Mr. Hyde

On the morning after the drunken skirmishes, Daddy always acted as if nothing out of the ordinary had happened. He was like a different person. But the rest of the family had an emotional hangover. I was perplexed by his Dr. Jekyll and Mr. Hyde personality, and wondered how he could forget or pretend to forget about the terrible things he had done. I didn't realize at the time that his blackouts prevented him from remembering the events of the night before. While my family still carried around their anger from the previous night, my father had by now transformed into a sweet, gentle and caring man. It was a kind and considerate father who dropped us off at the seven o'clock movie and promised through genuine smiles to be back by nine. But it was a snarling monster who returned at twelve o'clock or who never returned at all. Still, his gentle side appeared just often enough to keep my trust in him alive — trust that he would keep his promises and that he would eventually stop drinking.

It was his gentle nature that would bait the family into going out to eat at a restaurant. As if we had total amnesia of past experiences, we always looked forward to the event and the good time we would have. I wanted to believe that this time things would truly be different. But by the time we were seated, he would be drunk, bold, defiant and hostile. He would embarrass us with his coarse words and gruff manner. He insulted our waiters, and his loud voice and animated gestures annoyed those dining around us. Through exaggerated waving of his arms, he would knock over a glass of water or brush his sleeve through his food. His programmed response to our pleas for him to be quiet was a blunt, "I don't give a damn! I can buy this place!"

I would be so embarrassed and humiliated that I usually could not eat. It was not until I was 21 years of age that one night when this scenario was being repeated, I realized he might never change. I remember looking across the table at him as he made a spectacle of himself and wondering where that bright, capable man was whom I admired when his mind was spinning out inventions and dreaming new ideas. I loved that man but hated the monster that sat at the head of our table, boldly claiming he could buy the restaurant and every-one in it. Without saying a word, I left the restaurant before we were served and vowed to never eat publicly with him again until he was sober. That was the last public meal I ever had with him.

Despite all the bad times, though, my father was by nature a good man, loving and kind. I have many fond memories of being snuggled in his arms, listening to bedtime stories on cold nights. His train stories were the best, and I loved how he mimicked the chug-a-lug of the locomotive that lulled me to sleep.

He worked hard and always insisted on two things: that we brush our teeth before going to bed, and that we do well in school, striving for a good education. He was a good provider for his family. We never lacked for any of the material comforts, although we were not rich by any stretch of the word. Daddy frittered away most of his money on gambling and drinking, and our small house always showed signs of neglect. Still, we had the finest clothes and the newest cars, and he paid every penny of our college tuition for as long as we wanted to go.

We had one of the first television sets in our neighborhood. I remember that black-and-white small screen and "Hop-a-Long Cassidy," the first television program we ever watched. At Christmas it was a tradition for Daddy, hatchet in hand, to take us on a hike into the woods to chop down our own Christmas tree. "Store-bought trees are just not the same," he insisted.

I remember warm summer nights, the sight of fireflies lighting the sky, the deafening sounds of crickets and the slam of our screen door. Those were the special times.

A brilliant and resourceful man, Daddy was an inventor in his spare time. From my earliest memory he would sit in front of some contraption, contemplating the cosmos and staring into space. He only did this when he was sober and lucid. That's when I loved him the most. I could almost see his mind working, and I knew he was doing positive things.

He had mediocre success with a brand of curtain rods, trash can holders and a window-washing chemical that we bottled in a makeshift assembly line in our kitchen. One of us filled glass jugs with a powder and another filled it with water from the tap while another slapped on the label that read "Red-Head Enterprises" —

Daddy's affectionate way of acknowledging our behind-the-scenes help and his genetic gift of red hair to each of us. Those days were the best because we were doing something productive, good and useful. There was a sense of being a close-knit family as we worked together.

Daddy's biggest success came with the invention of a console-style beer can opener that was faster than the conventional hand-held type. It sold like wildfire and he made lots of money. He signed a contract with a major corporation in Chicago, which distributed his invention in bars throughout the United States and the world. His claim to fame came one night in a comedy skit on the "Dick Van Dyke Show." We all gathered around our black-and-white television set and watched Rob Petrie carry my father's invention around his office, trying to figure out what it was. Although it would later become obsolete with the advent of the pop-top can, revenues from sales became our sole source of income for years.

Looking back, I find it ironic that I spent my early teenage years working part-time in his small factory, manufacturing beer can openers. Little did I know that I was aiding and abetting on a large scale the very disease that strangled my family. Revenues from these sales not only paid my tuition through college, but also supported my father's drinking habit.

Childhood Trappings In An Adult World

I continued to carry my role as POW into adulthood although I no longer lived in a chaotic family. On my own, the need to control everything and everyone around me became an obsession. Things had to be done my way or not at all. But the old survival skills that saved me as a child no longer worked as an adult, causing me many problems in my interpersonal relationships at work, at home and at play.

As a grown-up, I had great difficulty with weekends and holidays when there was too much free time. Waking up on a Saturday morning with nothing to do made me panic-stricken. I felt out of control, as if something terrible could happen at any moment during those idle hours. I didn't know how to be flexible and live by the moment. I was afraid of the unknown.

Eventually I discovered that weekends were difficult for me because as a child, I never knew when a crisis with my father would erupt. Anytime there was quiet, it was the calm before the storm. If I let my guard down, the rapid-fire jolt of Daddy's inebriated outbursts would hit me like a jackhammer. So I learned to live with this uncertainty by always expecting the worst and staying poised for it, even when everything appeared calm. That way, I couldn't be caught unprepared. In adulthood I got into the habit of packing my weekends full so that I knew exactly what would happen next and how to prepare for it. There could be no surprises; I made sure of that. Although staying busy seemed to alleviate a lot of stress, it left no time for spontaneous, relaxing moments, no time for play and no time for smelling the roses and living in the now.

I carried the need to be responsible and plan things out into other areas of my life. I excelled in school and discovered that I could be academically successful and unconsciously hold on to my old survival skills. School helped me feel good about myself so I spent a lot of my time studying.

Three degrees and a doctorate later, I learned that the work world gave me the same sense of what I thought was fulfillment. I received my self-worth from work and it became my life. I transformed my long hours of study into long hours of work: evenings, weekends and holidays. I was hooked; I had become hopelessly addicted to work. I worked for the sake of work and the superficial, fleeting feelings of esteem and accomplishment it gave me. It also provided an escape so that I didn't have to deal with my feelings buried since childhood. It kept me disconnected from people and intimate relationships. At the same time, it gave me something with which to connect and with which to be intimate. Work was something over which I thought I could exercise total control, even though it actually had control over me. In work I had found my salvation, my Nirvana — or so I thought.

My behavior was highly rewarded in my job, and I quickly made it through the professorial ranks. But the other three-quarters of my life — social interactions, personal developments, and intimate relationships — suffered from neglect. I became obsessed with my career. I lived to work rather than worked to live. Like many children of alcoholics, work had become my bottle. I was driven. I had to have it. Like an alcoholic, I felt restless and became irritable when I went more than a few days away from my desk. Even when lounging on a tropical beach, all my thoughts centered around my next project.

Hardly a vacation passed that a stuffed briefcase of work didn't accompany me as part of my luggage. While others swam and played in the surf, I toiled over my word processor back in the cottage. My family became concerned, and after many stormy protests, work was no longer allowed on vacations. My response was what any normal work addict would do: sneak it into my suitcase. I hid my work as my father had hidden his bottle. When others strolled the beach, I feigned tiredness so that I could have a few moments of bliss alone with my addiction. It sounds strange now but at the time these behaviors seemed perfectly normal to me. Anyone who tried to interfere with my plans was immediately subjected to my harsh retaliation.

Father Knows Best

Many politicians, writers, comedians and entertainers (for example, Ronald Reagan, Carol Burnett, Jonathan Winters, Chuck Norris and Suzanne Somers) are children of alcoholics or CoAs. Many CoAs discover that as adults they are reliving the same destructive patterns of their families of origin (see Harry Crews, *A Childhood: The Biography Of A Place,* Harper & Row, 1983). Anywhere from 40 to 50 percent of CoAs become alcoholics themselves; others become work addicts as I did. One reason for this is that CoAs do not know what a healthy family is supposed to be like. Because of their early wretched family life, they develop unrealistic expectations of the ways families function. Many times they develop a fairy tale image and when the dream doesn't come true, they feel they have failed.

As a child, my vision of what a family should be came from the television shows I watched, "Leave It To Beaver" and "Father Knows Best." I dreamed of living in a beautiful house on a quiet and shady tree-lined street like the Cleavers or the Andersons. There would be peace and tranquility, and everyone would smile and talk instead of frowning and yelling. I would live happily ever after.

Needless to say, these unrealistic expectations were the source of trouble in adulthood when I was forced to learn that my family experience as a child and the fantasy of what my family should be were two extremes on a continuum, and that most families fell somewhere in between. It was a hard lesson to understand that it was okay — and even healthy — for family members to disagree. Also, on occasion, it was not out of the ordinary for family members to become angry or hurt, and to communicate these feelings to one another. But the main thing I learned was to keep communication lines open in a rational way.

Through years of hard self-inventory and the help of Al-Anon and Adult Children of Alcoholics groups, I came to see that my inner feelings and perceptions of myself had caused my life to continue on the same self-destructive course that began the day I was born. For a long time I had seen myself as a victim of an unstable childhood that had left me shy, insecure and basically unhappy. Viewing myself as powerless, bent and swayed by whatever life sent my way had become self-fulfilling.

The cycle of misery continued just as if my alcoholic father (who had died five years before) was still in control of my fate. The most important thing I learned in therapy and Al-Anon and from my own personal search is not to disempower myself. My approach to my upbringing became metaphysical. I no longer saw myself as a disempowered victim of an unfortunate set of circumstances. Once I learned to give up those feelings of victimization and to see myself as a person of worth and power, my whole life began to change. Using my childhood background as a transformational experience from which to learn, I began to reinterpret my life in a much more positive and constructive way.

Everything that had happened to me as a child had happened for a reason, both good and bad. I was a kid who grew up in an alcoholic home and it's a good thing I did because everything — I mean everything — in my life has led me to where I am right now. And I wouldn't trade my life for anything. I learned to separate abusive work habits from work effectiveness and become aware of the hidden motives for my work dependency. Now work no longer controls me or my life.

Saying Goodbye

My father became very sick with cirrhosis of the liver and leukemia. He died after five years of suffering and struggling with failing health. It was not until the day of his funeral that I put all the complex pieces of the puzzle together. I was able to resolve my conflicting feelings about him.

I sat alone by his coffin and looked at the tired face of a defeated man. For the first time ever, I saw him, not as my father, but as a fellow human being. I thought back over all the terrible times we shared together, and feelings of sympathy and compassion swept over me. Here was a man, born into poverty, who had a hard life — much harder than mine — and whose own father had died of tuberculosis before he was born. His life had been a perpetual struggle, mostly with downs but with peaks too. He had been a star basketball player in high school and had won several trophies. As an inventor, he had a great talent that never totally manifested itself. Somewhere along the way, consuming alcohol became his crutch to get through the tough times. But as is often the case, the tables turned on him, and it was he who was consumed by the alcohol, ultimately leading to his downfall.

I wept for the tragedy of a human life that never fully lived and the waste of talent that, going unnoticed even to him, fell short of flourishing. Most of all I mourned the relationship between father and son that could have been but never was. I did not shed a tear for and would not miss the man I knew as my father. But I yearned for the memory of the man who was never fully realized.

The Secret Is Out

My decision to write a book about work addiction is a meaningful communion between my personal and professional lives. It is a culmination of having lived in an alcoholic family and having worked for 20 years in the helping professions as a teacher, counselor, family researcher, therapist, and professor of child and family development. I wanted to share my personal experiences — not in a sensationalistic way but as a springboard for why I am who I am today and why I wrote this book in the first place. My hopes are that my life can be transformed into a positive experience for millions of other work addicts, many of whom also lived in chemically dependent families. This book is for them in hopes that it will touch their lives and help them in recovery. Like everyone else, I still have problems and concerns. But as a recovering work addict and adult child of an alcoholic, I have found, through extensive personal inventory and hard work, that life can be quite satisfying.

2

What Is Work Addiction Syndrome?

On a trip to Europe I met a couple from New York with whom I traveled for a month through Scandinavia and Russia. Because of his failing health, Alvin, the husband, had been told by his physician to slack off work. "You cannot change work habits," the physician told him. "But you can take long weekends and vacations." What this physician did not know, however, is that Alvin is a work addict. Long weekends or trips to far away lands are no antidote to his problem. Work addicts simply and literally carry their addictions with them wherever they go.

Alvin's wife Dolores says:

He's embarrassed for people to know it, but he has lugged his files all over Europe. But both he and I know that they will *never* be opened. I will not allow it! But he feels better just knowing they're there. He still hasn't unwound from the trip. He's been very uptight and compulsive the whole time. He works constantly. Even when we go to our mountain home in the Adirondacks, he must carry a portable phone with him in the boat when

23

he goes fishing. He is in direct and constant contact with the other attorneys in his firm in New York.

It's been a constant source of conflict in our marriage. When we'd take the children on picnics, I'd carry the blanket and picnic basket and he'd carry the briefcase. On trips I hit the museums alone while he works. It gets lonely.

The Disease That Kisses And Kills

Alvin has all the characteristics of a work addict. Most people are looking for ways to escape from work. Of all the addictions — food, sex, alcohol, drugs, spending money, gambling — why on earth would anyone choose work? Who in their right mind would want to work themselves to death? Who in their right mind indeed! No one. And that's what this book is all about.

Work addiction *is* a disease. It is the blessed betrayal. It's the only lifeboat guaranteed to sink. It serves you as a child when you're drowning in the disease of alcoholism or family dysfunction. You think you're saved. But you're taken hostage by a disguised form of the sickness that helps you survive, and then insidiously reaches out its hand and insists on your paying the price. My early days with a pencil and typewriter kept me from going stark raving mad. Unknown to me at age 10 and into my 20s, work addiction was already injecting itself into my life. It relieved pain, helped me forget, entertained me, offered me a sanctuary and gave me silent companionship when I felt all alone in the world. My greatest compulsions about work were the false sense of power and control I felt over my life.

But there always comes a point, usually in adulthood, when the same compulsive habits that saved you start to bring you down. Obsessed with my work, I slaved away nonstop — nights, weekends, holidays and even vacations.

"When I have finished my dissertation and doctorate," I told myself, "then I can relax." But I didn't. I had to write my first book and take that consulting job and this committee assignment.

Magnificent Obsession

Ten years later I had not taken a break. I had been in school my whole life since I was four years old in kindergarten. I went straight through for my PhD while holding down full-time, professional jobs. Since I was 20, I had never spent a Thanksgiving or Christmas Day without working. My colleagues and friends always looked forward to being off on those holidays. I thought they were lazy and felt contempt for them. I looked forward to the holidays so that I could be productive and show that I could outproduce them. During the holidays I would binge work on 12- and 15-hour days uninterrupted. When it was time to return to my regular job, I would have work hangovers. I was easily agitated, restless and mentally "spaced out."

On the day of my father's funeral, I continued to work uninterrupted in my office as if nothing out of the ordinary had happened. My presence in the workplace on this day of mourning was met with raised eyebrows, shrugging shoulders and one less subtle disapproving reprimand from a disturbed colleague. But my mind pretended deafness and blindness to any disapproval. It helped me deny the unusual nature of my behavior by reassuring myself that the only thing of consequence was finishing the report on my desk. Nothing else mattered.

I continued to take on additional consulting and writing commitments, committee assignments and civic obligations. I was a chain-smoking, caffeine-drinking wild man who thought he had licked his family disease. Everyone else was applauding me, so I must be doing things right. But why did I feel so miserable and lonely? Why didn't I ever laugh? Why wasn't life fun? Why didn't I have any close friends anymore? Why was my primary relationship falling apart? Why was I starting to develop chest pains, headaches, abdominal problems and allergies? If I was so successful and happy in everyone else's eyes, why didn't I feel that way inside? There is one answer to all these questions. I was work addicted.

I discovered the answer to the enigma when someone
very close to me entered a treatment facility for
alcoholism, and I went through the family treatment
program simultaneously. During my program, not only
did I realize I was the child of an alcoholic, but I learned
that I had been in a 15-year primary relationship with an
alcoholic, that I was co-dependent and that work had
been a blessing and a curse. It had helped me survive
childhood and young adulthood, but had become a noose
around my neck. It was slowly choking me to death.
With the help of Al-Anon and Adult Children of
Alcoholics groups, I have been in recovery ever since.

Work As Medication

Work abuse is a serious compulsive disorder. It is as
ravaging and insidious as alcoholism or eating disorders.
How many times have you been told, "Keep up the good
work?" And then there's, "Boy, is she dedicated!" or
"What a go-getter!" We all hear these accolades from
time to time on the job. Work addicts take them to heart.
Work is the drug of choice for many adult children from
chemically dependent and dysfunctional homes because
excessive work medicates emotional pain by making
them feel better. It can repress rage, hurt, fear, guilt,
sadness and just about any emotion. Work abusers get
hooked because work anesthetizes them from dealing
with unpleasant feelings that they have stored in their
bodies since childhood. Work addicts suffer some of the
same symptoms as alcoholics. They have similar denial
systems, reality distortion and need to control. Careers
zoom, and marriages and friendships falter because of
compulsiveness, self-absorption, overindulgence, mood
swings, and highs and lows. Work addicts get high from
work, go on binges and get hangovers as they ultimately
start to come down. The downward swing is accompanied by withdrawal, irritability, anxiety and depression.
Work abusers can never be fully happy, self-content and

peaceful until they face their neglected inner feelings without the medication of work.

The fact that Alvin was embarrassed about carrying a suitcase of work across the continent of Europe says a lot. He knew something was wrong. Instead of admitting it, he tried to hide it from others — everybody, that is, except his outspoken wife. Keeping the secret of work dependency is often part of the disease. It's really no different from alcoholics who hide bottles. As you saw from my story, I too used work in the same way an alcoholic uses booze. I was preoccupied with it. I binged and got high from it. I hid it from others. I sneaked and did it when others were not around. And I became agitated when I was prevented from working for long periods of time. Work addiction is based on a compulsive need to stay busy, to have a concrete feeling of productivity and to have others respond positively to you. It is hard for the true work addict to give up the habit.

In some ways overworking is harder to kick than the other addictions because it is the only disease that draws applause from others. Work addicts often have thicker denial systems than those suffering from other addictions because overwork is rewarded at every level of society — especially in corporate America. Work addiction destroys relationships and kills people. Amid praise and cheers marriages break, friendships dissolve, work effectiveness ebbs, and physical side effects and health problems appear. No one, least of all the compulsive worker, understands what went wrong. Amidst their crumbling world, work addicts drown their sorrows by rolling up their sleeves and digging their heels deeper into their jobs.

Low Self-Esteem And The Big Fix

Addicted workers do not overwork to provide for their families, to make contributions to society or to demonstrate loyalty to their companies. They overwork because they are obsessed. They overwork to fill a void that work can never fully satisfy. As perfectionists, nothing will ever be good enough. So they keep trying to do the task better because that will make them complete.

The attorney tells herself that winning one more case will put her on top. The university professor believes she will be revered in others' eyes after just one more book. The construction worker will have all the money he needs after building just one more house. The avid plant collector needs only one more rare orchid to make him happy for a lifetime. The interior designer needs just one more project as her crowning achievement. The actor only needs one more big role to make him famous.

They are the envy of their peers: accomplished, responsible and able to take charge of any situation. At least that's how they look to the outside world. Underneath the glitz and glitter of success, however, swirls an obsessive need to excel, a compulsive need for approval, a deep-seated unhappiness and a sense of low self-worth.

Feeling incomplete and unfinished, work addicts become work dependent to gain a positive sense of self-esteem they are lacking. They gauge the value they place on themselves through concrete results. They must be able to quantify their success through observable outcomes of "how much" and "how many." How many accounts they land, how many pieces of real estate they sell and how much money they make provide them with outward manifestations of their importance. Measured success comes from the competitive ranks of being top salesperson of the month to the more mundane acts of planting a tree, making a dress or painting the bathroom. When part of a compulsive pattern, all these acts convey the same message, "Look at me; I am worthy; I have value." Producing and achieving temporarily fill the inner emptiness and give work addicts a fleeting and false sense of self-fulfillment, until a day later when they need another fix.

They set themselves up for failure, though, because their standards are so high that no one could ever meet them. On the inside they feel like the small child who never does anything quite right, while harshly judging themselves for the most minute flaws. Why are they so hard on themselves? Because they feel badly inside, they try to "fix" themselves, to make themselves better — more finished, more complete. They refuse to allow themselves to make mistakes and, when they eventually do, judge themselves unmercifully. The cycle thus repeats itself as they delve further into work as consecration for their unforgivable sins.

Switching Addictions

As an adult child of an alcoholic, I prided myself that I never became addicted to alcohol "like my old man." Many adult children and children from dysfunctional families fool themselves into believing they have mastered the family alcoholism or dysfunction when, in fact, it masquerades as work. They often sense that something is wrong but cannot put their fingers on it. They may even boast, "I don't drink like my mom. I spend my time constructively, making worthwhile contributions on my job. I'll never be a drunk like her." Although many adult children convince themselves that they are in full control, they change addictions to cope with parental alcoholism, unaware that all addictions are part and parcel of the same disease package of co-dependence. Changing addictions into work is the best camouflage, yet most dangerous action for which little help is available.

Alvin left the dinner table and went to his room, saying he would return. He didn't. After a half hour, Dolores started getting uncomfortable. "I'd better go see what happened to my husband," she said despondently. She found Alvin back in their hotel room feverishly slaving away over his files. For the remainder of the trip, Alvin grabbed work in his room as often as he could. After two weeks into the trip, he was still tense and anxious, and only felt "right" when he was able to get to the suitcase of files that he dragged with him all over Europe.

Type A Behavior, Work Addiction And Workaholism

The denial of work addiction is greater in our society than any other form of addiction. If you check some dictionaries, you won't find "Type A behavior," "work addiction," or "workaholism" defined. We have not developed a language to properly refer to the problems of work dependency.

Even with the identification of the Type A behavior pattern, nomenclature was a problem. Cardiologists Meyer Friedman and Ray Rosenman, in their ground-breaking book *Type A Behavior And Your Heart*, described the Type A person as hard-driven, competitive, hostile and hurried. They invented the term because it was a new research area in which no one else could claim expertise, and it got them research grants to study the phenomenon. Type A behavior is considered a personality type that has most commonly been linked to heart disease. By contrast, Type B behavior types are relaxed, easygoing, and not overly ambitious or irritable.

In some ways the Type A personality pattern and work addiction syndrome overlap. They certainly share the same high stress level and the aftermath of physical and health problems. Both take a hard-driving, urgent and impatient approach to life. Many Type As are doubtless also work addicted, although there is no way to know how many. The biggest difference comes in the disease concept. Physician Ray Rosenman insists that Type A is not an illness, that it should not be changed, and that it is a perfectly normal way of response for some people. It's just their nature, so to speak. Work addiction, on the other hand, is a disease from which the dependent can recover. The work addicted learn their addictions over the course of years like alcoholics do, and they can unlearn them through a similar type of recovery program.

The term workaholism was invented as an analogy to alcoholism and refers to some people who behave with work as others do with alcohol. Despite this analogy, the way the term is used minimizes any hint of disease and perpetuates society's denial. The word is tossed around the office with cute abandon when employees want to bring attention to their tireless efforts. People casually refer to themselves as workaholic at social gatherings as something of which to be proud. Workaholism separates itself from the other addictions because it is viewed as a positive trait; whereas, alcohol and drug dependency, gambling and eating disorders are often considered character defects. Workaholism carries nowhere near the social stigma of alcoholism, overeating or any of the other compulsive disorders.

In today's work world, in fact, it is the "in thing" to be a workaholic. The Yuppie movement, with its emphasis on heavy socializing and heavy work, has made it vogue to be "upwardly professional." This faddish, here-today-gone-tomorrow trend, stresses material gain through hard work. This is very different from work addiction that is here to stay, regardless of society's whims, until recovery occurs.

To openly say one is an alcoholic at a social function would bring somberness and uncomfortable clearings of throats. To openly admit one is a workaholic, however, would bring chuckles. It is bad to be an alcoholic; it is good to be a workaholic. Alcoholism is associated with skid-row bums, instability and irresponsibility. Work is associated with purity, solidness and duty. You cannot do enough of it.

Because the correct choice of words is important for discussing addiction as a disease, I have chosen "work addiction" rather than "workaholism" because of the positive connotation attached to the latter term. The meaning of workaholism has assumed a tone of normality that is disturbing and has even been hailed as a positive addiction by management consultants. In her book, *Workaholics: Living With Them, Working With Them*, psychologist Marilyn Machlowitz claims that workaholism is as much a virtue as a vice. According to her introduction to the book, "There is no Workaholics Anonymous, nor should there be." (p. viii).

She insists that workaholics are surprisingly happy and are doing what they love (work). Superficially this may appear to be true because of the denial systems in place, but there is no such thing as the happy work addict. In fact, it's a contradiction in terms.

Work addiction more adequately conveys the seriousness of the disorder. Real work addicts will not brag about it, but workaholics will. How many people, for example, would openly announce at the company cocktail party that they're a work addict? It sounds too much like there might be a problem. It carries a less frivolous and more serious tone than workaholism, as it should. Although they cannot cut down, people who overwork, no matter how outwardly successful or happy they appear, are inwardly miserable.

Seeing the struggle Dolores and Alvin were still having after 40 years of marriage, I casually introduced the term "work addict" to Dolores one night after dinner. It helped her see her husband in a different light. "Work addict you call it? That sounds as if my husband's a sick man. That gives me a whole new way of looking at him — with more compassion and understanding," she said softly, looking into his eyes through the candlelight.

Healthy Work Habits Versus Abusive Work Habits

Most people overeat, overwork or drink too much at some point in their lives. Work addicts cannot be diagnosed by how much they work, alcoholics by how much they drink or food addicts by how much they eat. Just because the department store clerk puts in three or four hours of overtime a week, for example, doesn't mean he is a work addict. Although the amount of time spent is part of the overall puzzle, it is not the whole picture, just as alcohol and food addicts cannot be identified by how many Scotches or second helpings of mashed potatoes they have.

It takes multiple criteria to diagnose work addiction. Work addiction is a general approach to life that consumes the abuser's time, energy and thoughts. The major difference between abusive (or addictive) work and healthy (or constructive) work is the degree to which excessive work interferes with physical health, personal happiness or intimate and social relationships. Healthy workers give the amount of time and thought to their work that is proportionate to other activities in their lives. They enjoy their work, are productive and generally are effective in what they do. But they balance their lives with social and leisure activities, hobbies, and personal and family time. Work abusers cannot control their compulsive work habits and even use different words that reflect their true feelings about "the great divide:" work responsibilities and family obligations.

Generally, constructive workers are thinking about and enjoying the *now*. They're not thinking about work during off times. But addicted workers think about work all the time, and it takes precedence over and interferes with all other areas of life. The addicted worker is interested in "quantity control" while the healthy worker is interested in "quality control." The quality of work does not improve just because addicts spend more time at it. Overworking does not guarantee a high-quality product. Quality, in fact, can be negatively affected by overworking.

All addiction programs require abstinence from the drug of choice. For those who are chemically dependent, that means total sobriety because alcohol and drugs are not necessary for the body to sustain itself. But because even work abusers have to work and compulsive overeaters have to eat, abstinence for them requires avoidance from compulsive *overworking* or excessive *overeating*. Abstinence essentially means balancing with the other areas of your life the mental preoccupation, and actual time and energy devoted to these addictions.

Symptoms Of Work Addiction

Twenty symptoms of work addiction follow:

Physical Symptoms

1. Headaches
2. Fatigue
3. Allergies
4. Indigestion
5. Stomachaches
6. Ulcers
7. Chest pain
8. Shortness of breath
9. Nervous tics
10. Dizziness

Behavioral Symptoms

11. Temper outbursts
12. Restlessness
13. Insomnia
14. Difficulty relaxing
15. Hyperactivity
16. Irritability and impatience
17. Forgetfulness
18. Difficulty concentrating
19. Boredom
20. Mood swings (from euphoria to depression)

Are You Work Addicted?

To find out if you are work addicted, take the Work Addiction Risk Test (**WART**). The **WART** will help you measure your work compulsion. Once you have responded to all 25 statements, add up the numbers in the blanks for your total score. The higher your score, the more addicted you are to work. The lower your score, the less work addicted you are. The following key will help you interpret your score:

A score from 25 to 54 = You are not work addicted.
A score from 55 to 69 = You are mildly work addicted.
A score from 70 to 100 = You are highly work addicted.

The WART (Work Addiction Risk Test)

Read each of the 25 statements below and decide how much each one pertains to you. Using the rating scale of **1** *(never true)*; **2** *(seldom true)*; **3** *(often true)*; and **4** *(always true)*, put the number that best fits you in the blank beside each statement.

_____ 1. I prefer to do most things myself rather than ask for help.

_____ 2. I get very impatient when I have to wait for someone else or when something takes too long, such as long, slow-moving lines.

_____ 3. I seem to be in a hurry and racing against the clock.

_____ 4. I get irritated when I am interrupted while I am in the middle of something.

_____ 5. I stay busy and keep many "irons in the fire."

_____ 6. I find myself doing two or three things at one time, such as eating lunch and writing a memo, while talking on the telephone.

_____ 7. I overly commit myself by biting off more than I can chew.

_____ 8. I feel guilty when I am not working on something.

_____ 9. It is important that I see the concrete results of what I do.

_____ 10. I am more interested in the final result of my work than in the process.

_____ 11. Things just never seem to move fast enough or get done fast enough for me.

_____ 12. I lose my temper when things don't go my way or work out to suit me.

_____ 13. I ask the same question over again, without realizing it, after I've already been given the answer once.

_____ 14. I spend a lot of time mentally planning and thinking about future events while tuning out the here and now.

_____ 15. I find myself continuing to work after my co-workers have called it quits.

_____ 16. I get angry when people don't meet my standards of perfection.

_____ 17. I get upset when I am in situations where I cannot be in control.

_____ 18. I tend to put myself under pressure with self-imposed deadlines when I work.

_____ 19. It is hard for me to relax when I'm not working.

_____ 20. I spend more time working than on socializing with friends, on hobbies or on leisure activities.

_____ 21. I dive into projects to get a head start before all the phases have been finalized.

_____ 22. I get upset with myself for making even the smallest mistake.

_____ 23. I put more thought, time and energy into my work than I do into my relationships with my spouse (or lover) and family.

_____ 24. I forget, ignore or minimize important family celebrations such as birthdays, reunions, anniversaries or holidays.

_____ 25. I make important decisions before I have all the facts and have a chance to think them through thoroughly.

A score from 25 to 54 is a low risk score and indicates the absence of any compulsive work behaviors. You have few or none of the risk behaviors that could cause you physical or psychological damage from compulsive working. A low score in this range could even mean that you have healthy work habits and have achieved a good balance between work and other areas in your life.

A score from 55 to 69 means that you are somewhat dependent on your work for something that you are not getting in other areas of your life. You have some, but not all, the risk behaviors that could cause you physical and psychological harm. It could mean that you are building up to compulsive work habits that could become more serious in years to come.

A score of 70 to 100 means that you are highly work addicted and that you have all or most of the traits that put you at psychological and physical risk. A high score could mean that relationships with your spouse and friends are threatened, that you have already lost friends, or that a marriage or love relationship has dissolved because of your addiction to work. Your high-risk score also puts you at greater risk for stress-related health problems (such as heart problems or high blood pressure) and psychosomatic illnesses (such as head-aches, stomachaches, allergies or chest pain.)

Using The WART

You can use the information from the **WART** to help you reduce any risk that work abuse could bring to you. Read the test again and look at those statements you gave a 3 or 4 score. That will tell you a lot about how you're living your life. Ask yourself what steps you can take to reduce the risk involved in each situation by being able to honestly answer with a 1 or 2 score. Make each situation that you would like to change a goal to begin reversing your compulsive work patterns.

If you are truly work addicted, chances are that you will not be able to make these changes on your own, no matter how much you would like to see them change for the better or how hard you try. You can no more reduce or stop these behaviors than an alcoholic can automatically stop drinking or a compulsive overeater can stop overeating. The **WART** can help you see where problem areas are and set goals. But only a recovery program will help you lower your score. For now, use the **WART** to become aware of areas of concern that you would like to modify. You can use these areas of concern as a focus of change as you continue to read the book.

Common Characteristics
Of Work Addicts

As a group, work addicts share a number of common characteristics. It is not accidental that most of these same traits are shared with adults who grew up in severely dysfunctional and chemically dependent families.

Characteristics Of Adult Children Of Alcoholics And Work Addicts

The following traits are generally associated with adult children from alcoholic **and** dysfunctional families (as you note the comparisons in this chapter you will see that the similarities between them and work addicts are striking):

_____ 1. Guess at what is normal

_____ 2. Have difficulty in following a project through from beginning to end

_____ 3. Lie when it would be just as easy to tell the truth

_____ 4. Judge themselves without mercy

_____ 5. Have difficulty having fun

_____ 6. Take themselves very seriously

_____ 7. Have difficulty with intimate relationships

_____ 8. Overact to changes over which they have no control

_____ 9. Constantly seek approval and affirmation

_____ 10. Feel that they are different from other people

_____ 11. Are either super-responsible or super-irresponsible

_____ 12. Show extreme loyalty, even in the face of evidence that the loyalty is undeserved

_____ 13. Look for immediate as opposed to deferred gratification

_____ 14. Lock themselves into a course of action without giving serious thought to alternate behaviors or possible consequences

_____ 15. Seek tension and crisis, and then complain about the results

_____ 16. Avoid conflict or aggravate it, rarely dealing with it

_____ 17. Fear rejection and abandonment, yet reject others

_____ 18. Fear failure, but sabotage their success

_____ 19. Fear criticism and judgment, yet criticize and judge others

_____ 20. Manage time poorly, and do not set priorities in a way that works well for them

Legacy Of Adult Children

Guess At What Normal Is

Work addicts lose perspective on the normal balance between work and the other areas of their lives. Because they do not know their limitations, they drive themselves beyond human endurance. They put themselves under abnormal amounts of pressure by overdoing, overcommitting and overcompensating.

Have Difficulty Completing A Project

Because of overcommitments and spreading themselves thin, some work abusers are headed in many different directions at once. Their compulsions to push themselves and to impulsively jump in over their heads before plans have been thought through make it hard for them to complete projects in a timely manner. Lack of forethought often sends them back to clean up messes in their wake. They often inadvertently prolong and create additional work when they feel they are nearly finished with a project.

Lie Instead Of Telling The Truth

When it would be just as easy to tell the truth, they lie about the amount of work they do, sometimes hiding the truth from spouses, friends and other family members. They promise to cut down on the amount of work, but fail to keep these promises.

Judge Themselves Without Mercy

Work abusers judge themselves, colleagues and family members unmercifully. Their tendencies to overdo cause them to push and measure themselves, their children, other family members and colleagues against unrealistically high standards. When failure ultimately occurs, work abusers harshly rebuke themselves and others for failing to meet the standards of perfection that they have set.

Have Difficulty Having Fun

Restless and easily agitated, work addicts find it hard to slow down, relax, have fun and enjoy themselves. Even in social situations their thoughts are preoccupied with work and they remain uneasy, uptight and have trouble letting go.

Take Themselves Very Seriously

Work addicts take themselves too seriously because they learned in their early years that life is serious business. As children, they rarely get to enjoy the carefree world of childhood and grow up as serious little adults. Laughter and fun are exceptions to the general rule of the seriousness of getting the job done. People who "fritter" time away by playing and having a good time are considered foolish, frivolous and wasteful.

Have Difficulty With Intimate Relationships

The overabundance of work takes precedence over everyone and everything else in the lives of work abusers. Excessive work prevents them from forming and maintaining intimate relationships and close friendships. Overworking leads to losses in social contacts and relationships with loved ones.

Overact To Changes Beyond Their Control

The work addicted overact to changes over which they have no control, and struggle to control everyone and everything around them. They are uncomfortable in situations where they cannot maintain control of the circumstances. Trying to eliminate the unexpected and the changeable, they overplan and overorganize their lives through work so that conditions are predictable, consistent and thus controllable. They cannot be spontaneous or flexible because the fear of losing control is too great.

Constantly Seek Approval And Affirmation

They constantly seek approval and affirmation through work. Emphasizing productivity, they want something to show for their efforts, as well as a concrete manifestation of their self-worth.

Feel That They Are Different

They feel different from other people because excessive work isolates them and sets them apart. They feel that others do not understand the significance of the volume of work they accomplish.

Are Either Super-Responsible Or Super-Irresponsible

They are super-responsible when it comes to getting the job done at work but are often super-irresponsible when it comes to taking an active role in family life and keeping themselves healthy.

Show Extreme Loyalty

They are extremely loyal to their work, even in the face of evidence that the loyalty may be undeserved. Regardless of work conditions or salary scales, they are usually willing to do whatever it takes and to go the extra mile to get the job done, even when the company doesn't reciprocate with material rewards. They tend to work for the sake of working.

Look For Immediate Gratification

They must see the results of their efforts to know that they are involved in worthwhile pursuits. The overimportance they attach to the product versus the process provides that immediacy. Their obsessions to self-impose deadlines and to binge on work compel them to finish a project in a short amount of time rather than within more normal time frames.

Become Locked Into A Course Of Action

Instead of giving serious consideration to alternate behaviors or possible consequences, or waiting and planning, their need for immediacy often causes them to become locked into a course of action. They proceed with projects without giving thorough attention to details.

Seek Tension And Crisis

Work addicts seek tension and crisis, and then complain about the results. This is most commonly observed when they overcommit themselves or set unrealistic deadlines. They end up grumbling that they are overworked and have no one to help out with the task, even when they have refused to delegate or share the work load.

Avoid Conflict Or Aggravate It

Work is a sedative for addicted persons because it helps to keep them preoccupied so that they do not have to deal either with conflict within themselves or interpersonal conflicts arising in intimate relationships with friends and family.

Fear Rejection And Abandonment

Work abusers suffer from a deep-seated fear of rejection and abandonment. Through their unrealistic levels of perfection, they reject and put down those who cannot meet these standards; this is approximately 100 percent of the human population.

Fear Failure But Sabotage Success

Fear of failure is so great that it derails success. It becomes a self-fulfilling prophecy, driving work addicts so hard that they unwittingly sabotage their own success. Excessive work, with its overemphasis on quantity, often spoils the quality. It ruins the addict's physical and emotional health, and it cripples relationships with co-workers, families and friends.

Fear Criticism And Judgment

They have a double standard of work in which they severely judge and criticize others. Fearing the same harsh judgment themselves, they strive for perfection by becoming slaves to work habituation.

Manage Time Poorly

They manage time inefficiently by overscheduling and overcommitting so that they are constantly racing against the clock. They do not set priorities, such as personal or family time or time cushions built into their work days. Sometimes they seem to take the most inefficient avenue for completing tasks.

Major Signs Of Work Addiction

As grown-ups, many adult children develop some type of addiction. Those who do not use work as their drug of choice pass the disease of co-dependency on through one of the other major addictions. To recognize and intercept the problem of work addiction, I have organized the major signs around 10 broad categories that best describe work addicts. They are usually in a hurry, have a strong need to control, are perfectionists, have difficulty in relationships, binge on work, have difficulty relaxing and having fun, experience brownouts, are impatient and irritable, feel inadequate and are self-neglectful.

Hurrying And Staying Busy

Things never move fast enough for me. That's why I'm always doing three or four things at a time. There have been times when I've asked my secretary to do something, and she may not do it in the next 60 seconds. I have to catch myself because I think, "Why hasn't she gone to do that?" Then I have to tell myself, "If you want it done immediately, you have to tell her that, and you don't need it immediately." But just because it's on my agenda and it's my issue doesn't mean it's hers or someone else's. It's not that I get mad at her, I just think, "But why isn't she doing it?" Or I think about my supervisor and think I need to light a fire under him. "Why doesn't he see this as a priority?" Somehow I think if I dive in and do it my way, I'll do it better doing it my way.

Nothing ever moves fast enough for work addicts. They are haunted by a constant sense of time urgency and are always struggling against the limits of time:

> As I go out the door at home ready to leave, I think I'd better feed the cat or take something out of the freezer. I just try to cram in one more thing. I look at my watch and realize I have 10 minutes, so I'll put a load of clothes in the washer. While I'm in the basement, I'll pick up something and put it up. Before I know it, 15 minutes have passed, and I end up late.

Unless many things are going at once, work addicts are discontented. They usually have so many things to do, there are not enough hours in the day to finish them. Staying busy and keeping many irons in the fire become important ends to themselves. Conducting two or three activities at once is usual behavior. The faster work addicts can bathe, eat, get the kids to day care or clean the house, the more time they have left for additional work and the better they feel:

> I'll be talking to someone on the phone, filing my nails and thinking about what I'll wear to work the next day. I've read magazines at stoplights, or studied for a test, drunk coffee and eaten breakfast while driving.

Saving time is important in everything they do. Work addicts take short cuts wherever possible, sometimes even when it sacrifices the quality of work. The more work they can produce, the better they feel. A writer told his friend that he had signed five different book contracts. His friend looked at him in dismay and said, "You need to check yourself into a mental hospital!"

"Don't worry," the writer reassured him. "They're not all due on the same day."

The friend thought the writer's behavior was strange. The writer thought his friend's reaction was silly. He was addicted to work and didn't know it.

Need To Control

Work addicts have an obsessive need to control themselves and everything in their lives. They cannot and will not ask for help, preferring to do things themselves rather than share the work load. Many employers who are addicted to work do not want to give up control of situations, so they refuse to delegate authority to employees because no one else can do what needs to be done as fast or as well as them. Employers who do everything themselves get to maintain more control over the situation rather than handing the controls over to someone else.

The work addicted often get upset in situations where they cannot be in control or when things do not go their way. Being a part of group decision making where negotiation and compromise ensure that everyone's voice is heard, such as committee work, civic groups or a group of friends deciding on a restaurant, challenges the work addict's need to control. As a result work addicts are overworked, tired and overstressed. They often put co-workers in a double bind by denying them an opportunity to carry their share of work loads, and then resenting and complaining that they have to do it all themselves.

I found it interesting to watch a colleague who insisted on doing all the planning for an annual conference of which he was chairperson. When other committee members volunteered to help, he ignored their offers. Once he became overloaded, he vented his anger toward the other members, charging that they sat back while he did all the work. The inability or unwillingness to ask for help assures "quantity control" but not "quality control."

Work addicts tend to be more inflexible and rigid than most people, and they feel discomfort in spontaneous and unpredictable situations. Work makes them feel secure. It is the one thing they can control, or so they think, in an otherwise unwieldy life. Weekend lulls, where nothing is planned and the unexpected could happen, are traumatic for work addicts.

A university professor said that she remembered
leaving her office one Friday afternoon after a long, hard
week. With butterflies in her stomach, she wondered
what she would do during the weekend. At that point
someone handed her an announcement that grant
proposals were due in one month. Exhaling a huge sigh
of relief, she knew she had something to carry her
through another weekend, and calm descended over her.
She was like an alcoholic, bottle under arm, who was
assured of plenty to drink:

> For me work was an anesthetic. It was tranquilizing. It
> numbed the pain, calmed me down, helped me forget and
> made me feel good. Folding that three-inch thick
> computer printout under my arm made my adrenalin
> flow. That bundle was my security, promising to fill the
> hours, and give me purpose and meaning and self-
> esteem. Knowing what I'd do that weekend, I was in full
> control. But after the proposal was written, the empti-
> ness, unrest and depression returned.

Perfectionism

> Preferring to do things myself rather than ask for help
> is part of my perfectionist syndrome. You know that old
> phrase, "If you want it done right, do it yourself." If I do
> it, I know it's been done; I know it's been done completely
> and I know it's been done the way I want it done. If I had
> an employee that I completely trusted to do it the way I
> would do it, I would give up the task. I'd like to find a
> support person who could do as complete a job as I
> would. I haven't found one yet, although the people who
> work with me are very qualified and talented.

There is no pleasing the work addicted, no matter
how hard you try. As perfectionists, they complain
about small things. "Why isn't the house clean?" or
"Who left the cabinet door open?" or "Why isn't there
any soap?" At work they are grumpy when little things
are not perfect. "You typed my name without my
middle initial! You'll have to redo the whole letter,"
complains one compulsive worker; while another is

concerned about more trivial things, "The door to the supply room should stay closed at all times!" Work addicts are such sticklers that nothing can ever be perfect enough. They do not give either themselves or others permission to make mistakes. Making even the slightest error gives rise to self-recrimination. They hold high standards for themselves and judge others by those same inhuman principles.

An administrator shared his obsession for perfection:

> To an extent I think I'm superhuman. I've always taken on more than I was capable of doing, not that I don't have the ability. I just don't have the time. Physically within a 24-hour period, I don't judge my time well enough and always take on more. I'm obsessed with creating lists by which I live, finding a way to fill in any extra spaces or lines on them with obscure chores so that it will look like I'm busy. By virtue of my lists, I cannot be content to accomplish something without laying the groundwork for something else. Fearing idleness, I have to be striving to accomplish some kind of goal or some block of work.

Difficulty With Relationships

> My husband complained about me working in the evening. So I bundled up all this stuff, took it home, closed myself in my bedroom and worked on it into the wee hours of morning. I'd fall asleep with work piled on top of me. My husband would come to bed and find his side of the bed covered with ledgers.
>
> Finally he quit coming to bed and slept on the sofa. It was two years before I realized anything was wrong. When we separated, I wondered why I was crying about the bed being empty on the other side. I'd tell myself how dumb it was because he had been on the sofa for the last year anyway. I'd find myself almost falling off the bed, rolling over to try to find him there. I started purposely leaving books and stuff on his side of the bed, so there would be something there for me to cuddle with.

Excessive work interferes with intimate relationships and close friendships. Sometimes work addicts are dependent on others outside the workplace — usually a spouse, lover or close family member. All their thoughts and energies go into work, and little is left over for anything unrelated to work. As a result, they often appear helpless with small things and lacking in common sense. I was in my late 30s before I knew the difference between lettuce and cabbage, and I was in my 40s before I could tie a necktie. I was too busy working to take the time to understand the small things that get one through the day. As long as someone else was there to do them for me, it gave me more time to work. Learning to set a digital watch or to assemble a complicated children's toy can be bothersome because it takes precious moments away from more important work tasks.

On his trip across Europe, Alvin left all decisions to his wife. She kept his wallet and passport. She managed their daily visits to museums, tours and various sites. She computed the change ratio from dollars to rubles and made the actual exchange. Alvin dutifully followed her lead.

Accomplished in their chosen fields, work addicts can be klutzy at home and in the social world because they have put all their energies into work. Imbalanced, they have few social skills and few interests outside of work. Either their topic of discussion is work or they remain silent during social conversations because their narrow scope of knowledge prevents them from participating.

Overdependence on a loved one or friend strains relationships and causes resentments. The wife of a work addict told me she resented the fact that her husband prided his work but neglected their home life:

> The issue of control is a battle all the time. He's a perfectionist about his business. His condos are in such beautiful condition and look like model homes. If he gets a drop of paint anywhere it doesn't belong, he'll work hours to remove it. But our house is a dump if he has anything to do with it. He will not pick up after himself and he never cleans anything. Doing as little as he can,

he doesn't even take out the garbage. If I ask him to help me with something he gets sullen and withdrawn.

Neglect of home and personal life is the biggest complaint spouses have. A housewife told me, "I'm tired of sloppy seconds. After my husband finishes working, there's nothing but cold leftovers for me and the kids." Spouses feel secondary — even jealous and perhaps for good reason. They become suspicious that their mates are having an affair because of long and late work hours away from home. Even when no lovers are involved, spouses complain that there might as well be because the excessive work is just as hard to take.

The term, "wedded to work," was coined for a good reason, and it knows no gender boundaries. A female architect confided that, more than once, she mentally worked on a client's house plans during sexual intercourse with her husband. A gardener confessed that sometimes he, too, found himself designing landscapes while making love.

Work addicts put more thought, time and energy into work than into intimate relationships with their families, socializing with friends, hobbies, or leisure and recreational activities. They forget, ignore or minimize important family rituals and celebrations, such as birthdays, reunions, anniversaries or holidays. They cannot stop long enough to fully participate because such events require total immersion of the person at the expense of losing endless hours of work.

Some work addicts even use bargaining to get released from family "obligations." They might tell a spouse, "I'll go to the family reunion with you next weekend, if you'll keep the kids out of my hair this weekend so that I can finish this sales report." Such promises of cutting down on work or spending more time with the family are frequently broken. As the week approaches, there's more work to be done, and the work addict apologizes with, "Sorry, Honey. Looks like you and the kids will have to go without me."

When strong-armed into going on family outings or leisure activities, the work junkie does so dutifully but often begrudgingly. Their minds stay work occupied almost all the way. They pull every trick in the book to work during the course of the outing: "I gotta go make a phone call" or "I'll just read this report while we wait for dinner."

Work Binges

The work addicted rarely work shifts of eight-hour days, five days a week. They are usually still plugging away after their co-workers have called it quits. The golden rule of the work addicted is, "Do today what doesn't need doing until six months from now." They have trouble spreading their work over a period of time. They binge for days on a project until it is finished rather than complete it in small segments of time.

Travis, who is in the self-employed landscape business, works day and night for three days until he completes a project, rather than spreading it out over a four- or five-day work week. A community college instructor had the goal of completing all work on his desk until it was clear, no matter how long he had to stay at his office. The attitude of a healthy co-worker helped him rethink his compulsive attitude toward work: "There will always be plenty of work to do. No matter how hard and fast I work, I'll never really be able to catch up. So I just relax, take it easy and work steadily rather than try to stay ahead in this business."

Everybody has to overwork occasionally to meet deadlines. But when work addicts binge on work, they often do it because of self-imposed early deadlines, not mandatory time frames. A report may not be due for six months, for example. But a work addict throws a 12-hour marathon to complete it now, rather than complete it gradually over time. The concrete sense of completion is satisfying, and having the assignment out of the way early leaves time to focus on other work items. Sometimes their minds are not at rest until the project is completed, and they work day and night until it is done. An office manager work addict told me:

> My supervisor needs a report by Friday, so I'd better have it done by Tuesday, and typed by Wednesday. If I have changes to make or errors to fix, I can get it in first thing on Friday, and he won't have to call me and ask for it. I self-impose deadlines all the time. Because I'm rarely late, I usually give myself enough time to get where I'm going, even if it's across the street with time to sit and read. But I end up wasting lots of time that way; so if the meeting is at 1:00, I'll get there five minutes early. But I don't think anything's wrong with that. When I have projects that I have to submit to someone else, I work very hard so that I can get it done on time. The price I have to pay for procrastinating is unbearable. I go nuts. I panic; I can't sleep; I have such anxiety. Oh God! How will I get it done! Procrastination is a killer to me!

As the disease progresses, some work addicts conceal work from family and friends, sneaking it when they get a chance. Work goes everywhere the addict goes: in briefcases or luggage; for more serious addicts it goes under car seats, in glove compartments, in car trunks beneath spare tires, in dirty laundry bags or stuffed down inside pants and inside skirts. Some addicts work extra heavily after a quarrel or a major disappointment.

Kate's work obsession became her "weekend lover." She lied to her family so that she could rendezvous with work at the office:

> I would tell my family that I was going shopping on a Saturday and I'd end up in my office working. Or I'd tell them I was going to my girlfriend's house. After calling my girlfriend's and not finding me, they'd call the office and say, "I thought you were going to Dottie's." I felt like I had been caught with my hand in the cookie jar.

Difficulty Relaxing And Having Fun

> I always try to relax, but I don't relax very well. Sometimes when I'm exhibiting compulsive behaviors,

I'll tell myself, "Why don't you just stop and enjoy the moment. Live for the moment. Try it!" And I don't know what that means. I'm always in fast forward. Maybe I think I would be bored.

Restlessness is the hallmark of work abusers when they are away from their addiction. Why can't compulsive workers just relax and enjoy themselves? It sounds so simple, but it's not. The "Just Say No" campaign is useless with work addicts. Turning down work or cutting back on hours is like asking a heroin addict to refuse that next fix, the alcoholic to turn down that drink or a compulsive eater to forego that second piece of chocolate cake. It's just not that easy.

Many work addicts report a nagging voice in their heads when they try to relax or unwind. The voice (the disease) tells them that what they are doing is totally unproductive and a complete waste of time. "You will have nothing to show for this waste of time!" They start to feel guilty because they are taking it easy. It doesn't feel right. Becoming restless and even shaky, they start feeling useless and bad about themselves. They may even fool themselves that it is not their nature to sit still for very long. The guilt usually wins the battle when the addicted are not in recovery. They end up "white knuckling it" until they can get themselves out of the social situation and back into work. Work preoccupied, they take themselves too seriously, seldom laugh or smile and have difficulty having fun.

The spouse of a work addict described her husband's inability to let go and enjoy himself:

> It's really difficult to pull him away from any of his work activities. He gets really anxious when he's not working, and then I feel guilty if I try to get him to do something with me other than work. I wind up feeling as if I have deprived him of something.

Brownouts

A car swerves down the highway. The man behind the wheel is high but not from booze. He's high from work.

The man is a minister who is writing his Sunday morning sermon as he zips down the interstate. You've seen them before: motorists trying to read the newspaper, talking on the telephone or eating their lunch as they speed to get somewhere. When behind the wheel of a car, some work addicts actually put their own lives and those of other passengers in danger.

The work addicted suffer from something I call *brownouts,* in which they have memory losses of long conversations or trips to and from a destination because of mental preoccupation with planning and work. Brownouts are also a side effect of tuning out the here and now. Having lived in an addicted family all their lives, adult children learn that the now is scary, unpredictable and uncomfortable. Work addicts live in the future because of their undeveloped ability to live in the present.

Different from the fantasies of daydreams, brownouts result from work. One man told me, "My wife sometimes tells me she thinks I have Alzheimer's disease. But she doesn't have anything to worry about. It's just that my mind is on my work and nothing else is important at that particular moment. I'll ask her a question. And rather than wait for an answer, my mind has already jumped to something else. I'll ask the question again, and she'll say, 'Do you realize you've asked me that three times?' And I don't remember asking a question, much less receiving an answer."

Associates, friends and family members will often complain that work addicts ask the same question two or three times. If the question they ask requires a lengthy response, their minds jump to another thought without waiting to process the answer. Or they are involved in so many things at once that they do not even realize they have already asked the question.

A woman work addict admitted that her staff tells her that she has a hearing problem:

> They would say things to me while I'd be working on or doing something else. They'd be telling me about a

concern and I wouldn't hear them. Because something else had my attention, I'd tune out everything around me. Many times I'll be driving somewhere else and would end up at work. Because my mind is on five million other things, I get in my car and get on automatic pilot without thinking."

A University of Georgia professor also experiences brownouts while driving. She frequently finds herself in the middle of downtown, forgetting her destination. Her mind has been thinking about a problem with work or planning a special project. Once, while driving, she had been mentally trying to coordinate faculty course assignments for the next three academic terms. Suddenly she found herself pulling into the parking lot of a condominium where she had not lived for many years, and she didn't even remember driving there.

Another compulsive worker told me that while she was in bed she'd try to figure out how to solve a problem at work. Once, feeling thirsty, she went to the kitchen to get a glass of water. With her mind still on the problem, she returned to bed. Fifteen minutes later she heard the sound of running water. She realized that in her stupor she had put her glass under the spigot, turned and walked away without turning the water off.

One compulsive worker had spent a week's vacation with a family in Florida. One day after working on a sales report, he realized his wallet was missing. He had the whole family in an uproar searching for the lost wallet. They spent hours turning the house upside down, emptying bags of rotting garbage and filtering it through their fingers, opening drawers and searching under beds. He even accused the housekeeper of moving it when she was cleaning. They retraced his steps for ten miles by car, trekking in and out of stores, asking clerks and looking on top of drink counters in the 7-Eleven. Later in the evening he found the wallet right where he had put it, in a side pocket of his briefcase.

Work addicts spend a lot of time mentally planning and thinking about future events. Although present in body, their minds are often working while eating and driving, carrying on lengthy conversations or sometimes even during sexual activity. They have repeated episodes of forgetfulness because their minds are on completing the job, rather than the present moment. While healthy people pay attention to whom they speak to, where they put things and what they are doing at the moment, work addicts don't want to fool with taking the time to worry with those "unimportant" things that take a back seat to the work at hand.

Her husband's forgetfulness became a source of grave concern for the wife of this work addict:

> He's very forgetful. In fact, because I thought he might have brain damage, I started worrying about him. He forgets where he puts important things like the cordless phone. He's always walking around the house with it, and then misplacing it. Keys, checkbooks, bills and any items not nailed down get lost. But he never loses his work stuff. He knows exactly where it is. That's saying a lot because his office at home is really a mess. But he loses everything else.

Impatience And Irritability

> I have angrily left carts of groceries at supermarkets because they didn't have enough check-out people. Then I had to go shop again later. I don't tell people off or create a scene, line jump, stand there and stomp. But I'll make a conscious decision that the line is too long for me and these things are not worth the wait. I always have to be somewhere because I put myself on such a tight schedule.

Time is the most precious commodity of the work addicted. They do not like to be kept waiting. They are easily annoyed and cannot tolerate delays in grocery, restaurant or movie lines, or when waiting in doctors' offices. Many work addicts are deliberately late or get routines down to a science so that they will not have to wait.

A salesman who lives in Atlanta and has sales territory in Alabama told me how he gauges to the minute the trip from his house to the Atlanta Airport to prevent waiting. He leaves his house an hour before flight time. It takes 30 to 45 minutes for him to get there, and 10 to 15 minutes to park his car and check his bags. With this system he can walk up and be the last person on board because he "hates sitting and waiting for things." Instead of leaving an hour earlier that could prevent stressful hurrying, he says there are too many other things to accomplish in the extra hour that he cannot afford to give up. So he takes his chances that he will not get tied up in traffic and that the plane will take off on time.

Another corporate supervisor told me that she deliberately developed a pattern of being late so that, instead of waiting for someone, she could use that time to cram in more work:

> I'm always late. There have been so many times in my life where I've been on time and had to wait on people. In order to be on time, I had to stop something else that was important. I started consciously deciding to go five minutes late because I figured my appointment wouldn't be ready for me anyway. My first day on this job, I made it a point of being on time and ended up waiting for 10 minutes. I don't think I was ever on time again in six years.

More long-term waiting, such as waiting for someone to return a much sought after book to the library, can also unleash impatience and irritability. I realized I needed help the day I jumped down the librarian's throat about a book that had been checked out by another faculty member for the remainder of the term. On my second special trip to the library just to get this book, I was furious when told it was still unavailable. I demanded that she search the computer and tell me the person's name so that I could have a talk with him. She searched the name and looked sheepishly up at me from her terminal. "We're not supposed to give out that information, but in this case I think it's okay."

"Well?" I demanded impatiently.

"It says *you* have the book already checked out, Sir."

Needless to say, I was speechless and embarrassed beyond belief. The book had been in my possession for six months in a huge stack of other books in my office, and I didn't even know it. Somehow, waiting was always easier after that.

Some short-tempered work addicts become enraged over a minor disagreement. In their impatience they often interrupt others in midsentence to respond to questions or concerns that have not been fully verbalized. But if *they* are interrupted while in the middle of work, it's a different story. Nothing will raise the work addict's ire as such an interruption does. They even get irritable and depressed after a day or two in which they are forced to live without work.

Irritability and impatience are not always vented through full-blown anger. The wife of a work addict described how her husband sometimes expresses hostility through passive-aggression:

> He has a lot of passive-aggressive behaviors. His anger is indirect. He doesn't admit to being annoyed but instead acts sullen, with a facial expression that looks troubled. But if I ask him if he's bothered, he says no. Then he'll do something spiteful not very long after — something he knows upsets me — and then deny having done it to manipulate me.

When impatience leads to impulsivity, nowhere is the adage "haste makes waste" more appropriate. Important decisions are made and projects launched before all facts are gathered, before all options are thoroughly explored, or before all phases have been finalized. Results can be disastrous when the addiction outruns careful thought and reflection.

Kate gained a reputation at her job for taking something, going with it, and then going back and cleaning up
her tracks:

> I do that all the time. An idea will come to me and I'll
> say, "Ah! This is great!" And I'll jump in and go with it.
> I'll have it moving and be way ahead of everyone else.
> Everybody else is sitting back and taking it all apart and
> thinking through everything, and I'm way ahead of
> them. It took us two years to clean up the billing mess.
> Our billing procedures were behind because we were
> working so far ahead of ourselves. But I get high off it.
> "Why not make it happen, then we can go back and fix
> it," was the way I thought about it. We've got to keep
> the ball in the air or it'll die. If you let it go back to
> committee 15 different times, you've lost your spark.
> And it's not the same.

Self-Inadequacy

> I like to see progress. Of course, being in the people
> business and the education business, that's almost a
> contradiction in terms. You cannot be concrete when
> you're working with people. You have to be abstract. But
> there are other aspects of my job that allow me to see
> immediate progress. If I work really hard on a report, a
> letter or some type of document, no matter what, it
> always looks better when it's completed. I like to see the
> finished product. It has to do with the way I present
> myself as a manager to my supervisor, to my peers, to
> the people I supervise and to my colleagues in the
> community. I think a lot of that stems from the
> syndrome I grew up with: Be a good girl, do the right
> thing, follow the rules, do it right, make sure it's perfect,
> make straight A's, do the best you can, it better be good,
> make it look good and see the results. I'm very result
> oriented, which is definitely tied in with my approval and
> the rest of the world's approval. I used to say that I didn't
> care what people thought about me, but I really do care.

As I mentioned in Chapter 2, the work addict's sense
of inadequacy and poor self-esteem lead to strong
emphasis on production. Compulsive workers must see

the concrete results of what they do. They are often more interested in the final result of work than in the process. A work addict told me, "The only time I felt good about myself was when I was producing 'things' so that I could constantly prove that I was okay." Despite repeated accomplishments, addicted workers continue to feel badly about themselves. Work gives them a temporary high and feeling of self-worth. But one achievement after another is never enough. They are like alcoholics who drink to feel better, except they substitute work for booze. They continue to push themselves harder and harder, thinking that eventually they will gain their esteem, and be able to stop or, at least, slow down.

Aside from maintaining control, there are other reasons that the work addicted are unable to ask for help. The wife of a work addict told me that she believed her husband's inability to ask for help is also tied to self-esteem: "He never asks for help. If he was dying in the middle of the street, couldn't walk, and a million people passed by him, he wouldn't ask one of them for help. To me it seems as if he won't ask for help because he doesn't think he's worth helping."

Self-Neglect

I sure don't feel productive unless I'm working. When I get depressed, I get immobilized and paralyzed, just can't do anything, and feel helpless. At work you can't say, "I didn't sleep last night or I can't work today, I'm depressed." I've always had an insomnia problem, and there have been many times when I've gone three or four nights without sleep, but I still have to go to work. It makes me cranky, uncomfortable and grouchy, but nobody's going to say, "You don't have to go into work today; you stay home and sleep." That's not the way the world works.

Overwork leads to self-neglect, a host of psychosomatic complaints and physical health problems. Work addicts tend to ignore their own needs in favor of work.

They neglect their physical (nutrition, rest and exercise) and mental (play and recreation) health. Those who work in sedentary jobs are especially at risk. They may not get enough exercise, particularly if they work binge for 12 or 15 hours a day. Poor nutrition comes from grabbing fast foods so that they can work during lunch or skip lunch altogether. Accompanying addictions, such as chain smoking, caffeine habits and occasionally alcohol consumption, contribute to health demise. Constant stress that addicts impose on themselves from lack of recreation, sheer overcommitments, lack of sleep and overworking also leads to health problems.

Work addicts tend to ignore anything that distracts them from work, including warning signs of physical illness. When symptoms of health problems do appear, addicted workers are more likely than most people to let them go unattended, to deny their presence or to minimize their importance. They put work before everything else, even medical needs. They ignore aches and pains that could be telling them their body is tired or even in danger. Although a part of the addict's mind is aware of the problem, another part doesn't want to take the time to stop and think about it, let alone take the time to have it checked. Left unattended, these health hazards could ultimately cost them their lives. The work addiction of an insurance company supervisor caused her many health problems, but her story has a happy ending:

> I always had allergies and headache problems. Two years ago I developed this devastating stomach pain, with irritation and indigestion. I took the whole gamut of tests, and there was nothing there except damage to the lower end of the esophagus from gastric juice. My stomach hasn't hurt since I started walking in the evenings two months ago. That's made a significant difference for my stress management; I understand myself better and see what happened to me. I used to drink coffee all day long, but now I only drink one and a half cups a day.

Hope And Help For Work Addicts

As you have seen from these 10 characteristics, work addiction is a crippling disease. It is one of the most widespread and menacing medical and social problems of this century. And it is a disease that is difficult to overcome because it is not generally recognized by society or the addictive person as a legitimate problem.

Still, there is hope and help for the work addicted. With help, work abusers can rid themselves of the haunting problems of addiction. Those who identify with many or all of these characteristics may find comfort in knowing that they are not alone. This list can be a guide for personal healing. Those who learned these behaviors in a dysfunctional, unhealthy family can learn how to change them through a personalized program of recovery. Through recovery they can break the cycle of addiction and lead a happy and fulfilling life, without passing the dysfunction to the next generation.

4

Work Addicts Speak Out

I conducted a number of interviews with true work addicts and their spouses. The patterns I saw from one story to the next were amazingly similar. As you read the stories of the following people, you too will notice common threads interwoven throughout the case reports.

Denton

Denton is a 40-year-old school administrator for a large urban school system. He openly admits that work is first and foremost in his life. He discovered his addiction to work after three years in his own recovery from alcoholism. He scored 86 on the **WART.** He grew up with an alcoholic mother who, at age 73, had just started attending Alcoholics Anonymous five months before this interview.

> I have two jobs and I spend the majority of my waking hours taking care of the responsibilities and duties for both jobs. This is a pattern of behavior I've followed for years. But I've had no reason to change, even though I know something's wrong. I know I do things better, faster and more efficiently than most people can.

Most people with whom I have come into contact don't care or have the degree of concern for their jobs as I do. They don't view work or the responsibilities at hand as seriously as I do. Of course, I probably take them too seriously. If people are not going to do as well as I'm going to do, I might as well do the work myself.

Even in elementary school when a teacher would give an assignment, I would do more than what was required. If a report was to be five pages long, I'd do ten. If the teacher wanted me at school at 7:00 in the morning, I'd be there at 6:30 a.m. If the teacher wanted me to help with the erasers, I'd straighten the desk, do a bulletin board, help correct papers and stack textbooks too. I'd stay until the teacher went home, even if it was 5:00 in the afternoon. That was okay because I was doing what was right. I had to be the most outstanding one who did any task assigned to me. Then I could get the recognition that I felt I deserved for being the best and for all of the hard work and sacrifice I'd done.

As an only child, I never could predict what was going to happen. Because my father drank heavily on weekends and my mother drank all the time, I felt the need to overcompensate. I didn't want my life turning out as unpredictable and chaotic and lacking in direction and goals as theirs. I wanted mine to be more structured so that when all was said and done, I would have accomplished more than they did, and no one would view me as I view my parents.

From my early childhood, whether I was playing the piano, preparing a meal or giving a lecture, I had to be the best. If I made mistakes, I would find ways to punish myself so that I'd do better the next time. When I made errors I wanted to make sure I suffered for them so that they wouldn't happen again.

I must *always* be in the process of being productive — *all* of my waking hours. I cannot relax, but I wish I could. I like to see an effect that has come about as a result of my work because I know what I've done has paid off and was worthwhile.

I've allowed myself to take on more than I can reasonably do in the waking hours of the day, making me feel I am always behind. There are just not enough hours to accomplish things to the degree they need to be accomplished. I don't want to just scratch the surface of a task, I want to do it to the best of my ability. Although I know it's wrong, work always comes first, and my personal needs and activities always go to the bottom of my "list." I need to work on this weakness.

I'm a very goal-oriented person. I try to make the process bring about a better final result than what happened in the past. I like to take a situation, such as the method we used to take attendance in our 61 home-rooms. I want to take last year's way of doing it and fine tune it so we can get faster and more efficient results from the role taker of homeroom teachers. By working harder in the present sometimes you can limit the amount of work to be done in the future, and that will give you more time to take on more projects.

I sit at my desk in the mornings opening mail; my secretary brings in letters to sign; I have to dictate to her; I take care of several phone calls that come in while she and I are talking or shuffling paperwork; or another teacher will come to the door. At the same time I will drink my coffee, eat a snack and fill out a report that's due in the county office by noon. When I'm at home, I'm usually sitting at my desk, paying bills, talking on the telephone, eating dinner, running the computer and having the typewriter and computer printer going all at one time. It's just like a work factory.

I want people to leave me alone when I'm in a work mode; for example, I don't like to have discipline problems brought into my office while I'm in the middle of writing a memo. I want to do it at my time and at my pace. I have a tendency not only to do what's on my job description, but to create new duties and responsibilities to make it better than what the other administrators are doing. Down the road I get mad at myself for taking on more than was expected of me or more than I'm being paid for. Always doing more than is asked of me, I end up despising the job and everybody around; I have created a situation by taking on extra tasks that I don't need to do. I have lost control of my life, and when people ask me to go out, I am so bogged down with work that I cannot do both. I can't be social and be a work person. I cannot find the balance.

There's something in my body and my mechanism that keeps me moving. When I am fatigued and have had only three hours of sleep after staying up all night at the computer, something keeps me moving, even when there's no energy left. It isn't easy for me to give up, no matter what the clock says. I take a break to eat and try to work out once in awhile. But I usually don't stop until eleven or twelve o'clock at night, and many times not until two in the morning. Because I want to bear down on myself, I tend to put too much on my list, stay up past the time I should have and do projects that really could be done the next day. I want to make sure that I put forth some blood, sweat and tears so that I will remember that I've done the work and I did not come by it in an easy way.

A human being cannot accomplish all that's expected in education. As an administrator, I give more paperwork to my teachers and have to evaluate them based on it, as well as their classroom teaching. My job is overwhelming, frustrating and high pressured to the extent that I'm now looking for a way out. Having backed myself into a corner, I wish I could find a less stressful work situation. I have headaches almost every afternoon to the extent that I'm keeping Extra Strength Tylenol in business. I'm tired all the time but I don't allow the kind of rest I need. I haven't made time for it because there's too much work to be done.

I try to make everybody else do it the way I do it — to the degree of perfection that I do it. But people will only change to the degree to which they care about accomplishing the task. If someone rings up my groceries the wrong way, I irritably let them know that they have inconvenienced me by causing me a delay. I'll walk right out of the store, leaving the items on the check-out counter. On the other hand, I am usually the one to cause other people to be late. That's another pattern of behavior I really cannot explain. Even though I will go in early to do an assignment for someone else to gain recognition, get ahead or be successful, I have not been careful in controlling my own time when I arrive and when I depart. I have kept other people waiting many times because I have overscheduled myself.

Frequently, I have fallen asleep with my eyes wide open, looking straight at my secretary or another school colleague. I know they're talking, but my mind and body have gone on a short vacation. It's almost like I'm out of my body. Because I've overlooked my body, it says, "Hold on. I'm going on automatic pilot for awhile." It's a funny feeling.

My work has brought about the end of several relationships because after the newness wears off, I get back into my work. Although work has caused problems with my spouse, she understands and realizes my weaknesses when it comes to work. With unconditional love she accepts that this is the way I am at this point in my life. We both acknowledge that I need to change. I certainly prefer not to be work addicted, but I'm sure there's a solution. It's going to take a lot of time to get myself out of the situation that it took a lot of time to develop. Admitting the problem is the first step.

Kate

Kate is 50 years old and scored 81 on the **WART.** She works and resides in Little Rock, Arkansas, where she established and now manages a unit of a major urban hospital. Her father was an alcoholic who was often hospitalized, once for being wild, hitting a hole in the wall and shooting at Kate's mother during a drinking bout. He died when Kate was 13, the point at which she became a POW.

The last time I ever saw him, I remember him leaving that afternoon. He said, "Come tell me goodbye, I'm going to the hospital."

I was roller skating on the sidewalk. I said, "Are you sick?"

He said, "I am going in for some tests. When I come home, I'll buy us a TV." I kept on skating and he never came home. During the night, he was accidentally given a lethal dose of a sedative.

At that point I gave up my childhood. My mother took a second job. She was gone from early in the morning until late at night. I was 13, and I had two brothers, age 11 and six. My little brother became my baby. I got him up every morning, made sure he got his breakfast, made sure he had his lunch, made sure he learned to read when he came home from the first grade every afternoon. After picking him up from the babysitter after I got home from school, I helped him with his ABCs, made the beds and put on a pot of pintos. If there was any time left over, I went outside to shoot a few baskets with the boy across the street — my first boyfriend.

Three weeks after my dad died, my boyfriend committed suicide. I just kept right on trucking, doing all these things to keep my family going. Mother would come in at supper time, eat, tell me it was a good supper, and go to her second job. One day I made a birthday cake for one of her friends. She bragged on me to all her friends, "How many daughters at that age would think to make my friend a birthday cake."

I just sorta knew things had to be done and I did them. I had lost my dad, my boyfriend, my grandmother and my uncle all in six months. My world was falling apart around me, and by grasping onto those duties, I was able to gain control over my life. I could take care of my brother, clean this house, make this cake and do these chores that will make my world stable. And I have been doing them all my life.

I have been through crises that people wouldn't believe. People say, "How do you keep your sanity when your whole world is falling apart?" But that's the way I kept on going, to do what I could do well.

I didn't think I was work addicted until two years ago. It crept up on me. Out of a desire to do great things, I was a public health nurse. I would see three patients but I was bored. I thought, "Is this all there is?" So I got interested in kids in foster care and gave up my job. Day and night I was burning the midnight oil doing things for kids in foster care, writing letters to legislators, going to the general assembly, speaking in front of the Senate subcommittee on foster care — all of which consumed me with a fire. I was feeling good about doing it.

We adopted a couple of kids. Once they went to school I started nursing again and thrived on patient contact. With more and more office responsibility, I was stuck behind files of backed-up work two feet on both sides of my desk and on the floor around my desk.

I was managing a team of RNs. People were pecking at me all day long. "Can you do this?" "What should I do about that?" I helped people solve problems while all the paper work piled up. Then I started staying after five, trying to make a difference in the stacks. Some days I'd work from eight a.m. until eleven p.m. I thought the house and my two kids (one in third grade and one in eighth grade) were all right because my husband was there. I started working late because I wanted to get all this work done. Then after a while, it became the accepted practice. I didn't feel good not doing it. I never resolved the stacks. They were still there when I left that job.

My husband kept saying, "You're becoming a work-aholic."

And I said, "No, I've just got all this work to do." So I took a job establishing from the ground up a special hospital program. From the minute I interviewed, I thought I had the job. My wheels started turning and I couldn't sleep at night. All night long I was working at my current job — working on the backload of this stuff I had to do. But in my mind, I was already working on the new job. And I couldn't sleep at night. Finally, I put a yellow pad by my bed. Every time I had a thought, I'd turn the light on and write the thought down and maybe I could go to sleep.

My husband continually said, "You're working day and night. Can't you turn it off?"

"No, I can't turn it off," I told him. So by the time I got into the new job eight weeks later, I had policies written and all kinds of procedures in place for a job I had just started. My mind never stopped. It was like I was running on adrenalin. I didn't need to sleep even, maybe two or three hours of sleep a night. But I wasn't tired. I was having a ball and on a roll. I was so affirmed by the administration of the hospital, saying, "Hey this is great! You hit the ground running. We're up and making home visits in a month. Wow! I'm so impressed."

I was going to board meetings, and doctors' meetings telling physicians about the new program. All the affirmation stimulated me to do something else and it kept getting bigger and bigger. Finally I realized, "I'm doing it all." I did the payroll, policy writing, the billing and I knew the name of every patient. Only after I was separated from my husband did I realize I wasn't supposed to do all of this as part of the job.

My work addiction didn't cause our split, but it brought it to the forefront. In my absence from home, he lost interest in what he was doing as a househusband. He quit preparing meals or doing any household chores and got into activities that I thought were morally wrong.

One day I found out what my whole family and the rest of the world already knew. He had been inducted into the upper ranks of the Ku Klux Klan. Feeling betrayed, I knew I couldn't live with him anymore. He had looked for ways to feel some sense of power that he didn't have with his job loss or over me, and had found it in the Klan. I was off doing my own thing and growing, only acknowledging him through nagging.

My children knew what he was involved in. My husband had confided in them. They had got into a pattern of "Don't tell mother" because I was never there. I was so totally enmeshed in what I was doing that I wasn't reading the signposts. Looking back on every-thing, I should have known the day that he was inducted into the Klan.

When I finally realized I was away from home too much, I'd take work home. My kids used to take some responsibility at home, but they got tired of it. We used to have a neat and orderly house, even though it was never spotless. Later I forgot all that and the children lost interest because I would never see it anyway. I've actually stepped over dog excrement on my floor for days because I didn't have time to pick it up, and the kids weren't going to pick it up. Maybe some of the things that were going on at home were leading me toward workaholism. Maybe I was just escaping and that's why I became work addicted, rather than the other way around.

After my marriage completely fell apart, my 15-year-old decided to leave after an argument over rules we had. She went to live with her father, thinking the grass would be greener. One day after moving my office and the entire agency, I went home, and there wasn't a thing in the house to remind me of my family — no pictures, no nothing. She had taken all the little reminders.

Then I fell apart. I was as close to being shipwrecked as I've ever been in my life. But I was totally devastated because no more could I control anything. I was so physically exhausted that I started giving people at work the authority to do the things they knew how to do already. And the department is still running. We're as well off, maybe better, now that I have delegated some of the responsibilities.

When I became so emotionally drained that I had to detach from work, I was afraid it wouldn't mean anything to me anymore. After all, work was the one thing that had saved me for so long. I was scared that because I had removed myself from it a little, it might abandon me as everyone else in my life had.

Yes, it's hard letting things go. I don't let go of anything very well. That's why I had a hard time letting go of my marriage. I'm even a keeper of junk, and it's organized (it doesn't look organized) so well that I could go right now and tell you where anything is in the piles of stuff I keep.

One day I couldn't quit crying. And I called a friend that I'd known for 25 years at work. She said, "I'm on my way home. Come." So I left immediately. For two weeks prior to that I'd been giving away everything. I'd say, "Here, if you want a toaster, take it. Do you want some Tupperware, take it." When I got to my friend's house, I had a set of scales and said, "Here you can have these."

She said, "No, I'll borrow them but you've got to come back and get them in a few months." And I cried for two hours nonstop, laughing while I was crying. I stayed with her for three days, no toothbrush or anything.

Five days later, I was crying again. I was having to let go of everything. I told the ones I confided in at work,

"I've got a problem right now, you're going to have to take some slack." I was mourning a lot of things: a marriage, my childhood, giving up my job to others (which was very hard to do). But I don't take work home with me anymore because I haven't wanted to. Now I always do whatever needs to be done here at the office.

I'm aware of the fact that I've been addicted to my own adrenalin for a long, long time. I've been in addictive relationships all my adult life, and I just now realize what that is. Having that understanding helps me look back and see why everything happened and helps me understand myself better. As a result of that, I know how I can change some of those things. It won't ever happen to me again.

Sam

Sam is a 39-year-old adult child of an alcoholic father and scored 77 on the **WART.** His wife, Maureen, describes how his addiction to work is already destroying their 13-month-old marriage:

Sam's work is more important than anything else he does. The main problem living with a work addict is that it makes me feel secondary. He's involved in some aspect of work 12 to 16, sometimes even 20 hours a day, seven days a week. Aside from his full-time job with the city government, he owns two houses and three condominiums that he manages. He takes care of all the repairs and everything on the units. He is also president of one condominium complex. So he goes to those meetings and does the books. He'll get up, go to work and work eight hours. When he comes home, he goes straight to his study and works from six o'clock to eleven or eleven thirty at night. After a couple of hours of sleep, he'll wake up at one or two in the morning and work until five o'clock. Then he'll go back to sleep for another hour, get up and go to his regular job for another eight-hour day.

He's always busy and in a hurry to get things done. To me it seems compulsive. I think it's just the process of being involved in the work that gives him adequate distraction so that he doesn't have to reflect on himself or face other issues. I think it's a smoke screen. I think he's really depressed and doesn't know how to deal with it. He's worked compulsively all of his life, and it's a form of escape. He's not getting ahead financially, although he claims he's overworking for money. He savors every moment of the work process so that it never ends. When he's balancing books, he'll do some figuring or tabulating in eight hours that most people could do in one. It seems bizarre to me. Like people who eat too much, he has the same sort of intoxication with work that they do with eating.

Wherever we go or whatever we happen to be involved in, he's in a tremendous hurry to leave or stop doing it so that he can get back to work. There are no schedules involved nor can the work be measured from start to finish. The more he works, the more he wants to work. Like any addiction, the more he does it, the more he feeds his need to continue.

When it bothers me, I've said, "I wonder if you realize you worked 22 hours yesterday."

He'll think about it and say, "Well, maybe it was 18." When I present him with this information, he'll deny it even though it's plain as day. I've told him before that I feel real lonely, he never talks to me, he's real withdrawn, I don't feel like he loves me and I'm basically unhappy about it. He'll say that he's real sorry that I feel that way. But these are things that he has to get done and if he doesn't do it who will? He's got a semi-valid argument for doing whatever he does. But it's only because work is an accepted activity. He tells me that he was raised Baptist with the Protestant work ethic, which isn't something I would know about (because I am Jewish and because my father always had money). I guess putting the attention on my lack of understanding is his way of avoiding the problem.

One time, while upset and crying, I told him that I thought he was addicted to work. He said that there may be some truth to that. That's the closest he's ever gotten to admitting it. He thinks that working 20 hours a day and taking work on vacations is the usual. He thinks that these are his responsibilities and he's got to take care of them.

He spends so much time alone. At night he sleeps on the carpeted floor of his study. He says that he does this because it's too hot in the bedroom, even though the fan blows on him. I think it's just easier for him to get up in the middle of the night to work without bothering me. That way I won't know whether he's working or not. I think he realizes to some degree that his behavior is abnormal and excessive.

He looks for justifications to help him deny his extreme work habits. When we go on vacations he'll stay indoors and work, while I'm out by myself at the beach. I bring books to read, and he compares his working to my reading. It's like saying, "If you read books, then I can do work." I tell him I read to amuse myself and he says his work is a hobby for him. So I don't argue with him past that because at that point I realize that I cannot win.

He doesn't know the first thing about relaxing. He's very fidgety. He drinks a lot of coffee. When he doesn't have caffeine in his system, he gets a migraine headache. The headache gets so bad that it will cause him to vomit. His foot is always moving and he cannot sit still. He's often tired but he doesn't sleep much either because of insomnia. He's impatient with anyone or anything that stands in the way of his work, showing it through sullenness. He's especially impatient when I ask him to help me with something around the house. He's bored when he does anything that's not work related.

He ignored our first wedding anniversary. I gave him a card and asked him why he didn't get me a card. He said he didn't think it mattered to me. He doesn't pay any attention to other people's birthdays or special events. It would never occur to him to give someone a gift unless it is a season like Christmas. There is no such thing to him as a day without work, including Christmas and every other holiday. He forgets things that he told me and that I told him. Probably he didn't even listen to me when I told it to him the first time. He's just very senile acting some times. Other times he has responded to me in a way that is so inappropriate that I wondered if he was hallucinating. I have even asked him if he was hearing voices because his response was so inappropriate. I thought too that maybe he had a hearing problem.

For example, frequently I make an observation about something, and his answer has nothing to do with the subject, but addresses something in a totally different context.

I think he's distracted and 99 percent of the time he's not paying attention. He has disciplined his mind so that it stays on work as much as possible. Sam's always fantasizing about how he's going to do this report or that plan. His saying he has some thinking to do means he's preparing to withdraw. I don't know how much he's accomplishing. Sometimes I look at what he's done and it doesn't look like he's really produced anything. Nothing looks different on his desk. For all I know he's adding up the same column of numbers day after day.

Sarah

Sarah is 41 years old and came from a dysfunctional family. Although a work addict with a score of 78 on the **WART,** Sarah is in a 12-Step program for compulsive overeaters. She says she approaches life in a compulsive way that affects practically everything she does. Because work is a big part of everyone's life, she naturally transferred her compulsivity into the workplace. Sarah coordinates an office skills training program for disabled students in a large, urban community college.

I have a very strong compulsive nature and I have other compulsive behaviors — overeating, for example. I've always felt that I was excessive and intense. I'm an addictive personality and work is something I'm spending a lot of time on now. One does have a reputation to maintain. I don't want others to think I'm not doing a good job.

Part of my whole compulsivity is to do more than one thing at a time. For example, getting dressed for work each morning, I have a definite routine. I'm very methodical because when I wake up, I'm a slow riser and slow communicator but my mind is racing a mile a minute. I'm already so busy thinking that I have to depend on a routine to keep me on track and on schedule. While I'm cleaning my contact lenses, I'm thinking, "What else can I be doing to get ready while I'm doing this?" Or when brushing my teeth, I use a fluoride rinse that takes 30 seconds and my mind says, "Now, what am I going to do for 30 seconds?" That scares me because I know that's so compulsive. I guess productivity is the key and the fact that I don't want to get bored. Another part of it is that staying busy keeps me from stopping to think what's underneath all the frenzy, like what am I running from?

Starting when I get in the shower in the morning and on my way to work driving, I already have my priorities for the day in my head. Of course, I'm very much wedded to my calendar. I really live by that, which I don't mind. My "Day-at-a-Glance" is perhaps the most significant tool at work. I take it home with me; it goes everywhere I go.

Part of my relationship with my calendar is that I like to plan in advance. I use it as an aid to schedule activities. If I lost my calendar, it would cripple me. The few times I have either left it somewhere or forgotten it, I don't panic but am extremely annoyed. It's as if I have to backtrack because I don't want to miss an appointment, let somebody down, hurt somebody's feelings, fall down on the job, be unproductive or fail to follow the rules.

I'm one of those people who works better without a break. If I interrupt work, I lose my momentum. I'm much more productive and get more work done if I work four or five hours at a time. So when I eat lunch, I usually grab something around 2 p.m. or after. I'm glad I have the kind of job where I set my own schedule.

I have a compulsiveness to accomplish — productivity-related accomplishments. Sometimes at stoplights I read, file my nails, apply my makeup, put on my lipstick or comb my hair, clean out my purse, balance my checkbook or anything — anything just to stay busy. When I don't go out to lunch, I'll go get a sandwich on campus and bring it back to my desk. It usually sits there and I'll eat while I talk on the phone, write a memo or get something accomplished while I'm eating lunch.

I've always got some kind of work with me. I think it couldn't hurt to throw this report in with whatever I'm taking with me so that I'll have the security of knowing I will not get bored. Sometimes I get preoccupied with work and ask myself, "Did I already ask that?" I'm usually 60 miles ahead of myself on fast forward, thinking what I will be doing in the next 10 minutes, the next meeting, the next encounter, or what I have to do next or what and how much I have to do tonight.

I always stay at work long after my co-workers have gone home for the day, sometimes until 8 p.m. or later. I get this momentum going once the phone has stopped ringing, people stop dropping in, my meetings are over and I have returned all my calls. Then I can concentrate on paper work: reports, letters and policies. It's worth it to me to invest extra time, organization and energy after hours because the next day I am prepared.

The last thing of the day is to do a list for the next day's real priorities. I work long hours, sometimes on weekends. On my calendar I keep a tally of the hours I put in every day. My mentor at work told me when I started this job — because I was working 12- and 13-hour days — I was going to burn out. And I almost did. She said, "You keep track of those hours so that when you take 'comp' time, you don't feel guilty about it." I'm sure my overtime equals more than 40 hours a week.

I get real scared when I get behind. I had a recent situation where I was asked by the president of the college to chair a committee. There was a timetable for the mission of this committee. I got a three- or four-month late start. I thought "We'll never get that done." The appointment came at a very busy time. Even though this committee is very important, I had to perceive my job responsibilities as more important. I had to prioritize and I couldn't delegate this.

I worried about it so much that one night I woke up at midnight in a panic thinking, "I'm not going to get it done! They're going to think I've failed." It was terrible! It was the first committee that I'd ever chaired and I was afraid they'd think I had made a mess of it. This thinking was all projection. I told myself not to panic. I decided to schedule myself an hour for the next day and go to a quiet place and think this whole thing through and that's what I ended up doing. And it worked out fine.

Nevertheless I had terrible anxiety about it, and it kept me from sleeping two nights in a row. Other people would have said, "What? You couldn't sleep because of that?" But again, it's that message: Do a good job; be a good girl; and follow the rules. Your reward will be . . . who knows? I don't know what the payoff for this kind of behavior is — maybe it's the sense of accomplishment. But I'm not sure. When you find out, let me know.

Gloria

Gloria is a 30-year-old trainer for a major computer corporation. She trains internal personnel and sales people on new technology, products and markets. Her job is highly stressful and competitive. Her score on the **WART** was 81. She works between 50 and 60 hours a week and every weekend.

I've grown up in the culture of my company. I've been there for six years and it's always been as any high-tech company. It starts quickly, the technology is there, and it grows and grows. There are many high-energy people, and it's a young company in years and personnel. There are a lot of creative people, a lot of competition and many rewards from the corporation — nice recognition, bonuses and salaries.

I think you have to have a little work addiction in you to get ahead. One of the things we are told up front during the interview process is that this is not a 40-hour week job and that more is expected. If you have that drive and desire, you'll succeed.

Five o'clock means nothing in my office. Everybody stays and keeps working. People know what the unwritten rules are. Everybody has so much to do because there are several projects going on at one time. We're spread very thin. You're not forced to stay there. It's just that to do the job, you have to stay late. We do the jobs of many people, and there are a lot of deadlines. If I have to teach a class the next day and I still have deadlines, I have to stay. Some people in similar positions say, "What the hell," and they go home. But they don't last long. The nature of the job requires that to do a good job, you have to put in more hours than the usual eight to five. The whole industry is that way.

There is so much to keep up with that it's very frustrating. Sometimes I feel like I don't know enough to do my job because there's so much information that keeps me on my toes. I always fear that somebody else knows more than I do, and I feel depressed or guilty because I don't know as much as someone I work with or someone in one of my classes. As a trainer, I have to be aware of the trends in the market, which constantly changes because it's a high technology industry. Some software programs that are really hot at one point might just be a blank disc or have a newer version to replace it a year later.

I get in the office about 9:00 and stay until 6:00 or 7:00. I rarely go out during the day because it disturbs my day if I have to go out, even for lunch. When I do, it adds too much stress fighting lunch crowds and traffic. I usually eat at my desk and try and get some stuff done. I also do things while I'm on the telephone to business associates, like writing memos on the computer, filing something or reading something.

I stay booked up three months in advance. That's good because I always know what's happening. I know when I do or don't have any free time. Usually I don't. I'm never caught up. It's hard for me to relax when I'm not working. At home I feel very guilty because I've got tons of projects and the house is dirty. I feel guilty when I get home at 8:00 and become a couch potato. There are just so many things to do, I cannot lie around or rest.

I get upset with myself for making the smallest mistake. I learned a lot of this from my mentor. If something went wrong in the classroom, I'd just die inside. It was like how could you be so stupid. Now I'm learning to say, "Well, you screwed up. So what?" I get upset with myself because I think I should know better. If I screw up, I'll do it again. I cannot stand for that to happen.

I'm a real perfectionist in what I do. It's difficult for me to leave things to someone else because I have the feeling that they're not going to do it right or they're not going to do it the way I would do it. Sometimes I feel that it takes so much time to tell them what I want to do, it's easier for me to do it.

My job has to do with patience because I'm a teacher and trainer, and I have to have that attitude when I'm doing my job in front of the classroom. But with peers or other people I work with, sometimes I'm not very patient. The area I'm most impatient with is travel-related services. Because I travel a lot, I'm easily irritated with bad service: restaurants, hotels and airports.

The fact that I get upset when I'm not in control goes back to not trusting other people to do things for me. I also don't like people to make decisions for me. I'm a real snob about my company and my position there. I know what I need to be concerned with and what I don't. If I'm in a situation where I feel out of control, such as substituting for someone on vacation, I have a hard time with my self-image. I feel very intimidated.

When I first started this job, I got overcommitted myself because I wanted to make sure that I was cooperating with the efforts of sales marketing and learned a lesson from that. Now I can commit to more because I can put things together faster. When I overcommit, I end up working long hours and weekends to make sure it's the way I want it to be. I would be very meticulous about it.

Sometimes I get real high at work when I get recognition. It means a lot because I know I've done a good job. If I have done a class and it goes like clockwork, everything was perfect, and the evaluations were great, I feel high from that — very content, very excited and very happy. When you're in front of the group, it's like acting or performing. You get an adrenalin charge and your heart pounds because you are entertaining or teaching, and you're the person everyone is focused on. It is a physiological experience.

It's essential for me to see the results of what I do in some way. It's hard to quantitatively prove, but if I see a light bulb go off in somebody's eyes, or if someone says that he really learned a lot from one of my classes, it gives me a sense that I've done my job well.

If I can influence people and change their minds, it makes me feel good. That's really what my job is: to sell my company, our products and our services. Money and recognition are the best ways to motivate people. I have received a lot of recognition on the job, which is important to me.

It's difficult for me to go out and put myself into positions to meet people. Work has always been an easy excuse. I met my current boyfriend at work. He's somebody who understands what I go through at work, and what the stresses and expectations are. His understanding makes our relationship easier because we both travel a lot. On the other hand, there's another aspect of work orientation; often we talk about work and end up squabbling about it.

I don't have many friends other than those at work. There's a family culture way of life in my company. Everybody knows everybody. So I know many people. I know I should meet others and should participate in outside functions, but I don't.

In six years I've had five jobs with the company. Hiring is done within instead of from the outside. I've been in my current job for two years and I'm starting to feel the pressure from others around me who are getting into new positions. People are probably thinking, "Why are you still doing this? Isn't it time for you to move on?"

It's very difficult for me to start projects. When I do get started, I'm okay. Although, I have a hard time making decisions about how to execute the job. If I'm under pressure, there's no time to think about it. That's the way it is at my company. Orders from corporate may say, "You have to do this task immediately," or "This procedure has been changed and you have to do it the new way."

I don't have any hobbies because I don't have much free time. I've gained 35 pounds since last year. Some of it has to do with personal stress in my life but mostly because of my work and travel schedule. When I travel, I overeat because I may be stressed out about training in a strange place. When the training session is over, I eat because it's a reward. I've done a good job, and I can relax now. In the six years I've worked for this company, I have gained and lost close to 100 pounds. I must begin to plan time in my work calendar to do healthy things.

I've had chest pains that have moved down into my arm. A few weeks ago I was out of town doing some training. I thought I was going to have to stop because I started getting heart palpitations. I've had indigestion, stomach pains, stress in muscles in my back and in my sciatic nerve down my leg. When I'm under a lot of stress, ailments get worse. My body is sending me lots of messages that I need to listen to.

Eric

Eric, 27 years old, is a sales representative for a major national corporation. His job keeps him on the road most of the week and in his home office on most weekends. He scored 70 on the **WART**.

I put too much importance on work, but I'm real dedicated. My profession is the major focus in my life right now because I'm trying to launch my career. I'm trying to establish good work habits, and to develop some strengths and management techniques so that I can get ahead. I hope my obsession with work is only temporary. I have some goals set for my life that I hope will allow me to relax and spend more valued time with my family at some point. I hope that when I have teenagers, I will have established myself and reached a plateau where I don't have to work as hard to attain the same goals or make the same money.

The woman I used to date was not nearly as caught up in career life. Her life was social. She was very involved in wanting to go out, to be with people and to do things. She enjoyed sitting around gossiping with people and knowing what's going on in their lives. She would often say, "Don't go into the office today. Let's go do this or that." I'd tell her to do what she felt she needed to do but that I felt as if I had to accomplish these tasks. It became an irritant between us because she tried to convince me not to do what I wanted to get done. My attitude was, "This is obviously important to me or I wouldn't argue with you on this. So take it or leave it. This is the way it's going to have to be." She just accepted that this was the way I was, and she'd tell people that I was a workaholic. It was a sore spot for her, but she realized she wasn't going to change my mind so she left me alone on that.

I don't feel that there are enough hours in a day. I think I give myself too little time on jobs. I expect to work faster, and then interruptions throw off my schedule. I always blame myself for putting too much on my plate and not having enough time to complete the work. I'm constantly rushing, rushing, rushing to get it done.

I try to accomplish a lot of things at one time, otherwise known as multi-tasking. As a matter of fact, I keep a little note pad in my car and have been thinking about buying a dictaphone machine. My driving time is a waste of time. It takes me a minimum of two hours to get to my closest account and up to six hours to get to the one furthest away. I'm usually thinking and making notes as I'm going, which can't be safe to be sitting and writing while I'm driving. Now I have a car phone and spend a lot of time using it. I just can't concentrate on one task while I'm in the middle of it. I have to do other things as well.

I fill up my schedule, but generally run behind because I commit to too much, not allowing myself enough time to get it done. I rarely have to cancel something because I don't make it. I always accomplish what I set out to do. It's important for me to see the end results of what I do because it tells me that the job was completed. I don't have a problem turning things over to the people I work with as far as accomplishing the task. But I always want to know the result and to know that it was done satisfactorily. I don't care how they got there, but they need to have achieved the goal that I envisioned.

I don't know if it's necessary that I have to be in control, but I do get frustrated if I think my input is not carrying any weight. I don't mind working as a team member in a group, but unless I get equal time, I get upset. It doesn't necessarily mean that I have to control the outcome, but I like to feel that I at least have an active grasp of what's going on.

It's amazing that I can remember as many customer phone numbers, dates and professional events as I do. But I've never been able to remember my mother's birthday. I've been the best man for several friends' weddings. I can't tell you the last time I sent one of them an anniversary card. I just can't remember the dates. These events just aren't as important to me as my job. My motivation just doesn't come from being sensitive to those kinds of personal things. That's real selfish, but it's true. My motivation comes from my professional accomplishments, not from personal accomplishments.

5

How CoAs Become Work Addicts: The Cycle Of Addiction

Larceny is not a difficult crime to condone unless your childhood was the item stolen.

Pat Conroy, *Prince Of Tides*

Work addicts are not born that way. They develop work abuse habits over the course of their lives. These abusive habits begin in childhood as an extension of the disease of addiction that is passed on from one generation to the next. Switching addictions is the way many children cope with parental alcoholism and dysfunction. They dis-identify themselves from sick parents by switching to work and proclaiming, "It will never happen to me!" Although the work addiction takes a different form, it is part and parcel of the same disease package. Many adult children of alcoholics come to realize that they have repeated their parents' compulsive dependency but have camouflaged it through work.

Living In Inconsistency And Unpredictability

The inconsistency and unpredictability that typify alcoholic and dysfunctional homes are at the root of work addiction. All children must wrestle with some degree of psychological adjustment as they grow up, but the slings and arrows of everyday life carry a sharper sting in alcoholic and dysfunctional families. These families are characterized by constant conflict, quarreling and disruption. Household members are preoccupied with the alcoholic's erratic behaviors. Alcoholic parents use ridicule, rejection, harshness and mixed messages in their child-rearing practices.

Deidre's alcoholic mother beat her from the time the child was four years old:

> While she hit me she'd say, "You're a good little girl." How could I believe that? I remember she was on the couch, sandwiching me between her feet and the coffee table and pushing me hard against it with her feet. The whole time she was telling me what a good girl I was. I remember thinking, "Well, why are you doing that if you think I'm a good girl?"

Parental inconsistency and unpredictability are hallmarks of alcoholism that propel children into a cyclone of confusion. Children from these families learn early about the Dr. Jekyll and Mr. Hyde syndrome because their parents are notorious for making and breaking promises, and for mood swings during drinking bouts.

Nine-year-old Molly learned the hard way. Her alcoholic mother would beckon her with open arms, "Come here, Sweetheart, and give me a kiss. Mommy loves you so much!" Expecting to be comforted in the security and warmth of her mother's arms, Molly was met instead with a sharp slap across her face and a belligerent reprimand, "You are a bad little girl!" Molly never understood what she had done wrong nor what her mother meant by her negative comments.

Children often learn to cope with parents who have multiple personalities. They walk on eggshells and desperately try to second-guess parental expectations. But the consistency and orderliness of the outside world are absent at home. Rules, when they do exist, are switched around daily so that children never know what to expect.

Many children from alcoholic families have witnessed their parents out of control or violent in some way. Children themselves have been slapped, hit or thrown around. They live in constant fear of the next drunken rampage. The see-saw upbringing under the alcoholic parent arouses anxiety as children do everything in their power to change, so that their lives will become stable, predictable and manageable.

Trena said, "I thought that if I just tried to take some of the burden off my mom, that she would stop drinking. I thought that if I worked a little harder to keep my room clean, to make good grades and to help around the house, things would get better. But they didn't. Nothing changed."

Grappling For Control

The natural swing and style of all children is to make sense and order out of their worlds as they learn, grow and develop. When everything around them is falling apart, their natural inclination is to stabilize that world by latching onto something that is stable and consistent — something that will anchor them and keep them afloat in a sea of chaos, turmoil and instability. Out of their confusion and desperation, youngsters begin to seek control wherever and whenever they can find it.

For some kids that life raft is drugs or alcohol. For others it becomes food or relationships. For many it is productivity — usually in the form of schoolwork, housework or supervising younger siblings. This type of productivity is ultimately transferred to the workplace.

Sarah was enslaved by work compulsions at a young age:

> All my life I was conditioned by my parents. And when they stopped influencing me, I took it over myself — telling myself and conditioning myself. I've been compelled all my life to be a good girl, follow the rules and do the right thing. You have to make A's; you have to get a good report. And now I hear that echo in my head on the job: "Do a good job, do the best you can, make sure it's in on time. Make sure it's the most comprehensive and complete document you can provide. Make sure everyone is pleased with it." It's definitely tied into the "do the right thing and do it perfectly" syndrome.
>
> My deep fear is that somebody will tell me that I don't deserve to be manager or to get my paycheck, or that people will be disappointed in me. Boy, that's the big one. Or my supervisor will say, "Gosh, I thought you were doing such a good job. Now look what you've done!" I can't imagine that would ever happen. But my compulsive voice tells me that it could, so I'd better look out for it. Fear of failure, fear of looking stupid or fear of not being taken seriously are all carryovers from my childhood.

In order to "feel" truly stabilized and balanced, children put an overabundance of their energies into their life raft that appears to keep them afloat. As they begin to feel more and more secure with the false sense of stability, they clutch it tighter and tighter. Afraid to let go for fear of losing control, they become obsessed and compulsive. They go overboard with what has by now become their addiction. As children, they have embraced one disease in an attempt to escape from another.

Precocious Over Workers (POWs)

The acronym POW stands for precocious over worker; POWs are kids, who at a young age, already show signs of becoming work addicted. The acronym also alludes to the fact that they are hostages of dysfunction, forced to live in misery and despair. Although ultimately freed from their unhealthy, alcoholic home lives, POWs remain prisoners of work out of a need to inject control into an otherwise unsteady existence.

Common characteristics of POWs are:

1. They accept adult responsibilities for keeping the household running smoothly — such as cooking, cleaning and paying bills — before they are developmentally ready.
2. They assume the role of caretaker, at a young age, for the physical well-being, safety and care of younger siblings or of an alcoholic parent or both.
3. They are forced to deal with grown-up emotional worries and burdens that are usually reserved for adults on the therapist's couch.
4. They exhibit compulsive overachievement in sports, schoolwork, extracurricular activities and civic organizations, or in all areas of life.
5. They demonstrate precocious leadership abilities in the classroom and on the playground.
6. They strive to be perfectionists in their social behaviors and to gain adult approval by being "a good girl" or "a good boy."
7. They show the serious side of their nature, with a de-emphasis on relaxing, playing, having fun or enjoying the carefree world of childhood.
8. They develop early health problems that reflect stress and burnout.
9. They become responsible for being a symbol of their family's self-worth and identity.
10. They feel rushed to grow up too fast before they are developmentally ready.

Furthermore, POWs have feelings of inadequacy that are based on the sum total of all their childhood dysfunction. No matter what they did, it never made a dent in the family sickness. Nothing was ever good enough, so they kept plugging away to do better. The co-dependent parent, who was also consumed by dysfunction, never had time for them except to say, "Keep up the good work," "Do it right," or "I'm depending on you." The drinking parent unpredictably switched personalities at the drop of a hat and made promises but never delivered. The children felt guilt and blamed themselves for causing the drinking or dysfunction. Betrayal and hostility accompanied parental alcoholism. Embarrassment in front of friends and the family's tainted image are all internalized as part of the POW's personal identity. Shame and humiliation become part of the POW's self-concept, culminating in low self-worth. They use and abuse work (schoolwork, housework and ultimately job-related work) to overcome these feelings of inadequacy, making them feel better about themselves and giving them a sense of security and control over their lives.

Security is found in POW's unwieldy lives by their becoming the responsible one in the family. Although I called myself a POW, the role that I adopted in my family is also known by other names. Claudia Black calls kids like me "the responsible one" and Sharon Wegscheider-Cruse calls them "the family hero." Regardless of what terms we use, the patterns are the same. These kids are determined to show the world that everything is normal at home when, in fact, their lives are coming unglued.

My job was to perform so well that others would have to think that things were okay for me to be functioning so effectively. Like all POWs, I provided self-worth to my family, yet underneath the facade, deep-seated feelings of inadequacy and poor self-esteem predominated.

POWs are usually the oldest children who assume responsibilities for themselves and other family members. They take on such adultlike obligations as putting a drunk parent to bed after she passes out on the front porch steps. Or they may check little sister to make sure she has on matching socks before she goes off to school. In many cases POWs look after smaller siblings because their parents are psychologically and physically unavailable to them. At the tender age of 10 or 12, many POWs become parents to their younger brothers and sisters. I have even observed the blueprint of work addiction among young children of alcoholics as early as nine years of age.

At age 14 Fran had the look of a child who carried the burden of the world on her shoulders. She and her eight-year-old sister were frequently left alone by their addicted parents at all hours of the night. Fran, who had become the parent of the whole family, spoke openly about her parents' use of cocaine and alcohol.

> It makes me sick to my stomach when they get high. They smile and ask me if I want some too. I feel like they don't really love me because they'll let me do anything I want. I can go anywhere, do anything and stay as long as I want to. But I don't because there wouldn't be anybody to take care of my sister. I feel like I have to do it because they're too drugged out.

Nina, one of two siblings in a children of alcoholics group, was 10 going on 35. I asked her how things went during the Thanksgiving holidays. "Not so good," she replied. "My momma and uncle yelled at me because the turkey didn't turn out right." Asked to explain, she said, "I cooked the turkey too long and it was too dry, so they fussed at me. I just went into my bedroom and closed the door and hit my bed and cried."

I responded, "That's a pretty big job for a 10-year-old."

She looked at me as if I were half crazy. "I always cook Thanksgiving dinner, cause my momma's too drunk!"

Not only did Nina cook all the meals, but she also looked after her six-year-old sister and got her off to school every morning. She made breakfast, cleaned the house, did the laundry and any other chores that were necessary for her survival. Her sister clung to her during group; Nina spent most of her time parenting and

protecting her sister so that she missed the benefits of
the program for herself. During fun activities, Nina
reprimanded her sister for "acting silly" or "going the
wrong way in a game." She was always on the watch and
chastised her for such minor infractions as taking two
crackers at snacktime, instead of one. She could not
relax, play or enjoy the art and puppets because she felt
it was her duty to keep everything on an even keel. She
once told me why she did not laugh or play at home:
"Sometimes you don't play around an alcoholic because
like my mom, she'll think you're laughing at her, and
she'll knock your head off."

Nina and Fran are not children but overcompensating
adults contained in children's bodies. Robbed of any sense
of the security and safety, which should be the right of all
children, they have become parents that everyone in
their family relies on. They are likely to grow into the
kind of adults that everyone envies: being responsible,
achievement oriented, and able to take charge of any
situation and handle it successfully. At least that's how
they will appear to the outside world. Inside, they will
continue to feel like little girls who never do anything
quite right, while holding themselves up to standards of
perfection without mercy and harshly judging themselves for the most minor flaws. Convinced that they can
never allow themselves to depend on anyone, they will
inevitably carry a sense of isolation into their adult
relationships. Sadly, Nina might end up spending many
nights crying in her bed, pounding her pillow over things
far more important than dried-out turkey.

School is a breeze for many POWs because they are so
responsible, work so hard and do so well. They excel in
academics, athletics or both. They have an *overdeveloped*
sense of accomplishment, responsibility and perfectionism. Because achievement and competition are so highly
valued in our society, POWs usually go unnoticed and, in
fact, teachers and other adults reward them for their
compulsive drive to accomplish. They rarely know how to

play and relax, and become serious little adults. Their childhoods are filled with serious issues that are usually reserved for adulthood, such as, "I hope Mom doesn't pass out with another lit cigarette while I'm at school today!" While their friends are enjoying the carefree world of childhood, POWs worry about how things are going at home. These kids develop into adults who have difficulty trusting, being intimate and relinquishing control.

Sam, a 39-year-old man, never knew what it was like to be a child. He doesn't know how to play at all. His father was a physically abusive alcoholic, and his mother, a co-dependent addicted to prescription drugs. As the oldest child, Sam was the only responsible party in the house during his childhood years. From the time he was nine years old, Sam took care of his little brother. His father made him and his brother work when they were school kids at the gas station that he managed. They didn't get to play or have much of a childhood at all, and the household was at war most of the time. As an adult, Sam doesn't know how to enjoy himself. He cannot be playful, he has no favorite foods, he doesn't read the newspaper, he doesn't enjoy any kind of entertainment or going to the movies, and he doesn't even enjoy sex. It is as though he has no interests except for work. He doesn't have a good time doing anything. He's so stiff and rigid most of the time, his need for control is so great that he avoids situations where he has to behave spontaneously or act on the spur of the moment.

Hurried Children

Dressed to kill in makeup, heels, and blouse and skirt, five-year-old Heather walked into McDonald's with her grandmother and ordered a hamburger. An onlooker remarked, "Look at that midget!" When Heather was six, her teacher expressed concern to Heather's father that the child was not paying attention in class because she constantly pulled out her makeup and primped during lessons.

At age 10, Heather was on a diet so that her tight, designer jeans would fit a more shapely figure. A tall, large child, Heather looks more mature than she is. Her designer clothes, carefully manicured and painted nails, coiffured hairdo, jewelry, perfume and penchant for MTV and Sting deceptively mask her true age and act as a veneer of sophistication that hides her childlike confusion. She keeps a lot inside according to her grandmother; she appears very pensive, as if she is harboring secrets that she will not share, yet cannot handle either.

Exposed to things that many kids her age never experience, Heather had to grow up fast. At 18 days, she started her whirlwind growth when she was flown everywhere she needed to be — living with her grandmother in North Carolina for a year and then her grandmother in Virginia until she was three. At that time her parents finally set up housekeeping, moving into a Washington, D.C. condominium. After a year, the parents divorced, discussing the impending split in front of their four-year-old, who appeared to accept the divorce in stride. In the absence of her parents, however, Heather cried uncontrollably in her grandmother's arms. At four she was routinely placed on an airplane and flew alone to various relatives on the East Coast.

Academically Heather is pushed to read at home. Her parents buy books to encourage reading rather than for enjoyment. The 10-year-old has difficulty playing with others her age. In fact when she does, she takes the adult role of director, telling her friends what to do rather than playing like most other school-age children. From the time she was two, Heather was in nursery school and since school age she has spent after-school hours caring for herself at home alone.

The case of Heather illustrates the growing problem of what psychologist David Elkind refers to as *hurried children* — youngsters forced to grow up too fast. They grow and develop under pressure and are pushed to assume adult responsibilities before they are developmentally ready for these burdens. Most work addicts have a childhood history of some kind of adult responsibility ranging from caring for baby brother to making sure the electric bill gets paid each month because Dad is too drunk and Mom is too busy taking care of Dad. Like Heather they are thrust into a grown-up world with which they are emotionally and intellectually unprepared to cope. Not only do they acquire adult responsibilities, but they are recipients of the stress and tension that come with them. Young children of alcoholics are more likely than children of nonalcoholics to complain of stomachaches, headaches, sleeping problems, nervous tics and nausea, although no physical causes for these ailments can be found.

Many of the pressures from taking on the grown-up responsibilities of alcoholic parents — such as calling in sick to a drunken father's employer or making sure monthly bills get paid so utilities are not disconnected — can cause severe childhood burnout. Children who assume their roles of parent to a younger sibling (cooking, dressing, washing clothes and overseeing household chores) or to a parent (becoming Mom's confidant and helping her solve her problems of the bottle or becoming her protector by keeping a violent father from assaulting her night after night) must become little adults with all the worries and burdens. Ultimately, they miss childhood altogether.

Hurried children often have what medical scientists call Type A personalities that, because of being overly stressed and burdened, lead to physical health problems. Paul Visintainer and Karen Matthews of the University of Pittsburgh have traced the origins of the Type A behavior pattern and its association with coronary artery and heart disease to childhood. Type A children are descriptive of those children of alcoholics who, through their POW role, become compulsive overachievers and eventually work addicts. They attempt to control and suppress fatigue, are impatient, strive for competition and achievement, and have a sense of time urgency and perfectionism. Healthwise, this compulsive need to achieve in children is linked to such cardiovascular risk factors as fluctuations in blood pressure and heart rate. Visintainer and Matthews observed Type A characteristics among school children as young as five years of age, and these traits endured over a five-year period.

Carl Thoresen in his research at Stanford University found that Type A personality parents pass these behaviors on to their children. Parents who were rated as "high Type A" tended to be more controlling and dominating, and gave specific directions and criticisms to their kids. Their children turned out to be more competitive, angry and highly stressed than children whose parents did not impose pressures to succeed. Although Type A children struggled and worked harder, they did not accomplish any more than children who approached tasks with a more calm and relaxed style. Overall, Type A kids were more anxious and unhappy with themselves and their relationships than non-Type A children. The numbers of Type A children who come from chemically dependent families are unknown. The similarities, however, between behavior patterns of Type A kids and the compulsive overachievement behaviors of many children of alcoholics are striking.

The box contains the Matthews Youth Test for Health (MYTH), which was developed to distinguish school-age children with Type A from Type B behaviors (youngsters who do not exhibit Type A traits). The child is rated on how characteristic each of the 17 items is on a scale from 1 (extremely uncharacteristic) to 5 (extremely characteristic). Possible MYTH scores range from 17 (extreme type B) to 85 (extreme Type A). You can rate your own child or another youngster in whom you are interested to check for the possibility of any early compulsive work habits.

The Matthews Youth Test For Health*

1. When child plays games, he/she is competitive.
2. This child works quickly and energetically rather than slowly and deliberately.
3. When this child has to wait for others, he/she becomes impatient.
4. This child does things in a hurry.
† 5. It takes a lot to get the child angry at his/her peers.
6. This child interrupts others.
7. This child is a leader in various activities.
8. This child gets irritated easily.
9. He/she seems to perform better than usual when competing against others.
10. This child likes to argue or debate.
† 11. This child is patient when working with children slower than he/she is.
12. When working or playing, he/she tries to do better than other children.
† 13. This child can sit still long.
14. It is important to this child to win, rather than to have fun in games or school work.
15. Other children look to this child for leadership.
16. This child is competitive.
17. This child tends to get into fights.

*Reprinted from K.A. Matthews and J. Angulo, 1980. "Measurement of the Type A Behavior Pattern in Children: Assessment of Children's Competitiveness, Impatience-Anger, and Aggression." *Child Development* **51**:466-475. Used with permission of The Society for Research in Child Development.

† The scale is reversed for these items.

The Invulnerable Child Myth

During the 1980s social scientists identified and began studying the phenomenon of *invulnerable children* — those reared under the most dire circumstances who somehow grow and develop remarkably well despite their disadvantaged surroundings. Also known as "resilient children," the most common characteristic of these kids is their ability to cope and react to stress in exceptional ways. Even though they are reared in extremely traumatic and stressful dysfunctional and alcoholic homes, they are described as stress-resistant and are said to thrive in spite of these disadvantages.

Resilient children are said to share a number of common traits. They have good social skills. They are at ease and make others feel comfortable too. They are friendly and well-liked by classmates and adults. They have positive feelings of self-regard. And they sense a feeling of personal power for influencing events around them. This contrasts with the feelings of helplessness of vulnerable children. Not only do invulnerable children feel in control, but also they have an urge to help others needier than themselves. They are successful, usually receiving high grades in school. And as adults, they become high achievers in their careers. Their early family misfortunes fuel the flames of motivation instead of destroying their intellectual and creative potential. Invulnerable children, in fact, are said to thrive on the early turmoil in which they live.

Invulnerable children sound like carbon copies of POWs. On the surface these kids appear to function exceptionally well, despite their dysfunctional upbringing. Outwardly, they appear to have it all. They may be the most attentive, the most dependable, the smartest and the most popular children in school. They follow the rules, always finish their schoolwork in the allotted time and often are leaders in school governments and extracurricular activities. They make the best grades and are sticklers for getting their work in on time — sometimes even before it is due. They can be the president of the student council, star quarterback or homecoming queen.

But they are by no means invulnerable. Underneath the facade, a different story unfolds, and herein lies the danger of the invulnerable child myth. Many cases of invulnerability are disguised inner misery that children are compelled to hide. Since they are more adept at most things, it is only natural that they would be more skilled than most children in hiding their pain. These "resilient" kids may, in fact, be in greater need of help than kids who can reveal their vulnerability.

As Claudia Black noted in her book, *It Will Never Happen to Me*, "The majority of these children simply do not draw enough attention to themselves to even be identified as being in need of special attention. They are a neglected population. If they are busy and look good, they will be ignored."

Their childhoods are filled with serious issues ordinarily reserved for adulthood. While their friends are playing and enjoying the carefree world of childhood, POWs dwell on their parent's drinking and welfare. Their resilience also conceals inadequacy and poor self-esteem. Underneath their success and achievement is an obsessive drive to excel at everything they attempt and a compulsive need for approval, deep-seated unhappiness and a sense of poor self-worth. These children browbeat themselves into perfectionism, refusing to allow mistakes. They are overly serious, have trouble having fun and judge themselves unmercifully. They learn to take control of everything around them to keep their world from coming unglued when their parents drink. Their "invulnerability" becomes their compulsion and prevents them from becoming intimate with others.

Because achievement and competition are so highly valued in our society, these children go unnoticed and, in fact, are rewarded for their compulsive overachievement. The myth of the invulnerable child feeds the denial of the disease of alcoholism, encourages children's dysfunctional behaviors, and instead of helping them in their recovery, perpetuates their demise.

I used to think I was an invulnerable child, called myself that during public speaking engagements and was even written up in two child development textbooks as a classic case. But that was before I knew I was the child of an alcoholic and before I knew anything about how alcohol and dysfunction affected my childhood. Praise from teachers, neighbors and even relatives who admired and rewarded my "invulnerability" only drove me further into self-misery, feelings of inadequacy and eventual work addiction. I always thought it strange that I could be so perfect in everyone else's eyes and still feel miserable inside. The truth is that I was vulnerable after all. I just was clever enough to make everybody think I was invulnerable. My school and career success actually came about as a result of my being a POW from the time I was 10 years old.

Middle Childhood

Developmentally, there is a natural time in the life cycle when all children struggle with the same emotions that children of alcoholics experience in greater intensity and depth. The first patterns of work addiction appear in the developmental period known as *middle childhood*. This is a sensitive time when youngsters are more susceptible to developing the dysfunctional behavior patterns associated with adult work addicts. A number of developmental factors naturally occur among children universally at this age (anywhere between six and twelve years) that could lead to work addiction. Two chief ingredients, concrete thought and emphasis on productivity, form the foundation for later work abuse. These two natural developmental milestones prime children from dysfunctional and alcoholic homes for work addiction.

Concrete Thought

Middle childhood opens the door to thinking. Before ages six or seven, thought is illogical, magical and fantasy oriented. It is based mainly on trial and error, and a series of hunches and guesses. But a shift occurs around age six or seven in which children enter a period of *concrete thought* — in which logical thinking appears but is limited to concrete or actual objects. This age is a natural transition time when children mature mentally and use reasoning. This new way of thinking is partly biological and partly learned. Because their reasoning is still tied to the concrete, children find it necessary to have tangible objects (as opposed to abstract processes) so that they can understand what they are learning and doing, and can have observable results from work efforts. At this age, children love to collect and classify things. They enjoy making objects, and because of their concrete form of thinking, like to have observable objects to think with and to represent their efforts. Coincidentally, this is also the age when children start school, where productivity and accomplishment are emphasized.

The period of middle childhood is universally known as "the age of reason." Among many cultures of the world, this is a time when children become caretakers of younger siblings while parents work. In India and other parts of Asia, Mexico, Africa and North America, children are expected to care for themselves to some degree as well as supervise younger brothers and sisters. Twelve-year-old Nyansango girls from Kenya, for example, are put in charge of their baby brothers and sisters until the children can walk alone. They must feed, bathe and watch over themselves as well as their siblings while their mothers work in nearby gardens or go to the market. Developmentally middle childhood is a natural time that children, regardless of their culture, are expected to assume some household and child care duties. For children in alcoholic and dysfunctional homes, however, these responsibilities are multiplied by emotional frequency and intensity.

Industry Versus Inferiority

During middle childhood, all children enter a stage of personality development called *industry versus inferiority* in which success arouses feelings of productivity and competence, and failure arouses feelings of inadequacy.

Whether a child develops industry or inferiority is strongly influenced by the support and feedback that comes from important adults and peers. Resolving this conflict is necessary for healthy and productive work habits in adulthood. For children of alcoholics, the crisis at this stage is multiplied, and passing the test much more difficult than for children from healthy, functional families. Feelings of worth and industry come when children's efforts and products are recognized and approved by others. Accomplishments come from doing well in school, learning new skills such as playing musical instruments, or achieving distinctions in Scouts or other civic organizations. In alcoholic and dysfunctional homes, children can never do enough or be good enough to stop their parents' drinking or erase the family dysfunction. But this is the age that kids keep trying. At this age they try to rescue the family through the natural way that is available to them: by overachievement. But no matter how hard they try, it can never be enough to cure the family of its disease. We find these adult children still plugging away, at ages 40 or 50 fixated at this stage of productivity, trying to save their families of origin.

When frequent failure or disapproval is common, as in most alcoholic homes, children may come to believe that the results of their work are not worthwhile and that they themselves have low self-worth. Poor work habits and feelings of uselessness are sometimes the consequence. Some children from alcoholic homes get stuck in this stage and spend the rest of their lives trying to prove to others that they are competent and worthwhile. They become overly serious and do not know how to have fun. Achievement becomes a compulsion; external accomplishments become sources of self-esteem; and they may become high achievers in school. Compulsive patterns become more defined by ages nine and ten — the same ages at which children's denial systems become firmly cemented. The need for concreteness through productivity is arrested in POWs, while healthy children resolve these issues by about age 12. POWs carry inferiority, thinly veiled with a need to be industrious into adulthood where they become prized work addicts in their chosen careers. The addiction whips them into submission and enslaves them for life, becoming full-blown work addiction in the workplace. Inside they feel driven, unhappy and worthless. Although their standards are unrealistic, they judge themselves and others harshly for not meeting them. Nothing they accomplish can ever be good enough to change these inner feelings of incompetence — except for the completion of a good recovery program.

Children Of Work Addicts: Breaking The Cycle Of Addiction

As parents, work addicts are psychologically unavailable to their kids. They generally do not take an active role in their children's growth and development. When they do, it is often to make sure that their children are mastering their parents' perfectionistic standards. Child-rearing expectations are so unrealistic that children of work addicts are doomed to fail. And when they ultimately do, they internalize that failure as poor self-esteem. They feel incompetent and unworthy, and that something is wrong with them for not being able to meet their parents' expectations.

Passing On The Perfection

A 43-year-old woman whose mother was a compulsive worker said that as a child when she did something wrong, her dad would get over it right away. But she had to win back her mother's approval. Her mom gave her the cold shoulder for a long time until she proved she could be the perfect little girl. Today that perfect little

girl is addicted to men and dependent relationships. She
continues to get herself involved with men who psychologically reject her. She relives her relationship with her
mother many times over by making herself a doormat
for the men she dates so that they will love and approve
of her. She attends Co-dependents Anonymous to help
her learn how she can break the cycle of addictive
relationships in which she continues to find herself.

Living with a work addict, whether as a child or a
spouse, is very difficult. Everybody in the family is
negatively affected by the experience. It is hard to say
who suffers the most, but for youngsters the major
disadvantage is that there is nothing obvious to point to
as the reason for the confusion, discontent and frustration that children experience. If Dad drank excessively,
the child could point to the bottle. If Mom was strung
out on pills, the drugs explained her unusual behaviors.
But the Puritan work ethic prevents us from faulting
our parents for hard work. In fact, hard work is a sign
of fine, upstanding, righteous people. So the logical
conclusion that many children of work addicts gain is
that there must be something wrong with them. They
are not good enough because they cannot measure up to
their parents' standards of perfection.

Work addicts are determined that, as parents, their
families will not function in the chaotic and dysfunctional
ways that their childhood households did. In the case of
42-year-old Irene, her parents both had been raised in
alcoholic homes. They wanted to make sure that Irene
and her brother would have it better than they had had
as children. Alcohol was never around as Irene and her
brother grew up. Instead, her mother became a placater
and her dad, a family hero. Irene's father was such a high
achiever that he got his "thank you" notes out the day
after Christmas. He held high standards for himself and
naturally for his children. If he could do his best, then
everybody else should do their best too.

There were lots of "shoulds" in Irene's family. Her
father was a traveling salesman on the road; because he

constantly worked much of the time as she was growing up, she saw him mostly on weekends. Her parents never wasted time; they were forever busy and doing. Everybody in her family was always trying to do everything right — anticipating anything that could create trouble before it happened. They operated from avoidance of conflict. When she was a little girl, Irene's father gave her a dollar every time she read *How To Win Friends And Influence People*. Says Irene, "That book emphasizes the people-pleasing stuff — tuning into others and making them feel important. Now I understand that underneath all that kind of manipulation is the basic need to control how others feel about me."

Irene remembered that there was a sense of something missing as a child. She always wished there was more closeness in her family. She always thought it was her fault that she was so unhappy and lacking as a child:

> My dad was a good provider, a regular churchgoing man. My parents worked hard to provide for us and to send us to summer camp. They wanted to be Ozzie and Harriet, and they tried real hard to be. But I never felt loved and accepted, even though I know my parents meant well. So with such a perfect upbringing, there had to be something wrong with me for wanting to have intimate, feeling conversations and relationships, and for feeling like I wasn't loved or accepted.

Work addicts pass on the disease of co-dependence to their children. Being in control, being perfect, doing what others want you to do and measuring your worth by what others think — all constitute the personalities of children of work addicts. The way to have self-esteem is to be good, to be right, to do well and to be perfect. Children of work addicts may not turn out to be work dependent. But chances are they will develop some type of compulsive behavior that will cause them to have difficulty in their lives and to pass the disease on to their own offspring.

In Irene's case, she became a compulsive overeater:

> When my dad got angry, he got cold and sarcastic. I didn't know how to deal with it. I would have rather been beaten. My response was to be crushed inside and not to react in a way that would let him know that I was hurt. I ate a lot and became overweight to deal with my stuffed feelings. It was also a form of rebellion for me because my eating was an issue with my dad who'd say, "Oh, you're having more potatoes?"

For much of her adulthood, Irene had no recognizable conflict in her life. She bypassed conflict by being accommodating to other people. Being accepted and understood became her major coping devices — being a good girl and good daughter, and doing all the things she was supposed to do. Being the child of a work addict made her a placater. She was willing to forfeit her own wants and needs by yielding to the whims of others. Meanwhile, she stuffed herself with food to fill that same void that her father had tried to fill all his life with work.

Irene's parents obviously had her best interests at heart. We all want the best for our children, and most parents do their best to see that children get what they need. But unless the cycle of dysfunction has been broken, parental perceptions of "the best" are limited, defined and distorted by the disease that is inadvertently transmitted to kids, despite parental efforts to the contrary. As an attempt to "dis-identify" with their work-addicted parents, children often switch addictions; yet the disease continues camouflaged.

Sarah, who is recovering through Overeaters Anonymous, had a mother who was a compulsive worker:

> We used to have this joke around my house, "There's three ways to do things: the right way, the wrong way and Thelma's (my mother's) way," and now I think that about myself. "There's three ways to do it: The right way, the wrong way and Sarah's way." At work I take

my perfection very seriously, but in my domestic life, my standards have become slack. I think part of that is related to the fact that I lived in a house where you'd throw Kleenex in a wastebasket, and my mother would empty the wastebaskets three or four times a day. Now all I have to answer to is me, and I don't care if the house is dirty because I'm too tired.

Breaking The Cycle

There are a number of things work-addicted parents can do to avoid leaving their offspring with a legacy of dysfunctional behaviors. First and foremost, of course, is to get help from one of the 12-Step programs, such as Al-Anon, Co-dependents Anonymous, Adult Children of Alcoholics groups, or from one of the other programs for specific addictions. Positive changes in parents will automatically filter down to all family members during the normal course of daily interactions. Chapter 8 gives detailed steps on how work abusers can balance their lives and start the recovery process.

Aside from personal recovery the following guidelines are suggested. Try practicing them on a daily basis with your children.

1. Love your children unconditionally. Set reasonable limits on their behaviors, but never withhold love as a punishment for children's mistakes.
2. Encourage them in their successes and enjoy their successes with them, but let them know that it is acceptable for them to fail and that they do not have to be perfect in everything all the time.
3. Be there for children after a big failure, wrongdoing or letdown. Help them understand and accept that failing is part of being human. Allow children to make mistakes and help them to see their mistakes as learning experiences. Teach them that no one is perfect and that they do not

have to be super-responsible.

4. Avoid hurrying children. Let them grow and develop at their own unique pace, according to their unique developmental timetable.

5. Present your children with challenges and encourage them to face challenges that match their developmental abilities, but help them learn not to bite off more than they can chew. Avoid unusually high expectations and burdening them with adultlike responsibilities, even when they are eager to accept them.

6. Encourage your children to balance their lives with work and play. Make special efforts to provide them with opportunities for a lot of playing. Play is the work of young ones and is at the very root of everything that they become.

7. Let your children know that it is okay for them to relax and do nothing. Some of our fondest memories are of our childhood play experiences. Reassure them that they do not always have to be producing a product to please someone else, but that it is acceptable to please themselves and that can include doing nothing.

8. Validate your children for who they are and not just for what they do. Provide unconditional support for them as individuals — not support for what they produce or accomplish. Let them know that you accept them, regardless of whether they succeed or fail. Value them and hold them in esteem by letting them know they are special even when they are not producing a concrete object.

9. Have reasonable expectations based on what children are capable of performing at their respective ages. Take into account individual interests and personalities of children.

10. Let children have some daily and flexible schedule at home with free time built in for choosing activities that match their interests. Teach them

to build in spontaneous and spur-of-the-moment activities from time to time. The best way to teach this, of course, is by example.

11. Protect children from the harsh pressures of the adult world without overprotecting them, and give them time to play, learn and fantasize.

12. Provide children a peaceful and pleasant home atmosphere, shielded from excessive marital disputes and involvements in parental conflict.

13. Try not to pass needless stress and worry on to children. Give them opportunities to talk about their own worries and stresses. Adults can save theirs for the therapist's couch.

14. Guide children toward wise decision making by introducing limited choices that match their emotional maturity.

15. Reward children for their triumphs and successes, no matter how small. Let them know you love them and are proud of them for who they are, not what you want them to be.

16. Always start the day on a positive note with pleasant words and calm routines.

17. Plan special times together each week as a family (without television), and listen to what your children have to say.

18. Refrain from burdening kids with adult responsibilities of raising a sibling, keeping house and having the emotional worry of being a parent at age 10 or 12.

19. Provide children with parental guidance when they must make significant and difficult decisions that would benefit from your input.

20. Avoid modeling your family after "Ozzie and Harriet" or "The Donna Reed Show." These are fantasy stories that, in the long run, create more problems for children who fail to learn that all "normal" families have problems and conflict that can be resolved through healthy communication.

21. Refrain from making snap judgments and criti-

cizing children unnecessarily.
22. Focus on children's positive actions rather than always harping on the negative.
23. Limit the amount of work you bring home in the evening and on weekends, and save some of that time for special moments with your youngsters.
24. Give children opportunities to play, relax and have fun with other youngsters their age rather than spending their time with adults in adult activities.

Pressures to accomplish, succeed and please others cause kids to miss the experience of childhood. Time to play, learn, fantasize and enjoy the carefree world of childhood is the right of all children. Through a searching and fearless inventory of their clash between work and child-rearing practices, work abusers might uncover subtle influences of how their children are adjusting. Guilt, worry and uncertainty may be the overriding emotions of many work-addicted parents. But rechanneling these feelings into positive actions can improve the quality of life for them and their offspring.

The period of childhood, compared to adulthood, is the shortest time in the life span. Some children burn out or drop out before they have lived through this brief period. Childhood is the foundation for adult lives, and youngsters who have a chance to be children will become healthier, more well rounded adults and are less likely to mourn their losses later. Parents can provide an enriched environment where children can experience the wonder and magic of childhood, learn in a positive way from their own mistakes, and grow and develop at their own rate. Once this is done, parents should give themselves a break, worry less and make the best of child-rearing practices for their own and their children's mental well-being.

7

Work Addiction
In The Workplace

Often, persons who come from dysfunctional families find organizations repeating the same patterns they learned in their families. Even though these patterns feel familiar, they do not feel healthy.

Anne Schaef and Diane Fassel
Addictive Organizations

Addictive Work Settings

The editor of a major publishing company offered me a large sum of money to sign a book contract because she said, "I know you're a workaholic like me; you'll live up to your commitments, and get the job done right and on time." A few years ago, I would have been complimented by her comment. But as a recovering work addict, I was horrified that my disease would make me so attractive to others, especially corporate America. My abusive work habits were clearly seen as a benefit, not as a disadvantage.

Although corporate America traditionally has valued and perpetuated work addiction, the types of dysfunctional environments that it creates are rapidly coming under fire from critics. Authors Anne Schaef and Diane Fassel reveal in their book, *Addictive Organizations*, how business and industry encourage the denial of work addiction, and actually promote it as acceptable and preferable because it appears to be productive. The authors suggest that American work organizations function as individual active addicts by denying, covering up and rewarding dysfunctional behaviors among their employees. They show how dysfunctional managers and those in key corporate positions negatively impact the organizational system and the employees of that system. My interviews support their view that nonrecovering addictive and co-dependent employers are re-creating their dysfunctional family patterns in their work environments.

The dysfunction created by work addiction pollutes the work environment, generates stress, lowers morale and throws the entire organization off kilter. The roles that workers grasp so that they can survive the chaos become roadblocks to productivity and quality in the work force. The following list is a profile showing additional problems generated by work addiction in the workplace:

1. Low morale
2. Disharmony
3. Interpersonal conflict
4. Lowered productivity
5. Absenteeism
6. Tardiness
7. Job insecurity
8. Mistrust
9. Lack of team cooperation
10. Loss of creativity
11. Stress and burnout

The Company Workhorse

Once they grow up and enter the work force, POWs encounter their greatest difficulties. They usually become highly successful in their chosen careers and, like the corporate executive, quickly climb the ladder of success. But they pay a huge price for their overdeveloped sense of responsibility and accomplishment. Obsessed with the need to control and manage people and things around them, POWs become full-blown work addicts and put their own feelings and needs on hold. This creates problems with being intimate and developing healthy interpersonal relationships.

Many jobs that require creative problem solving operate on the premise that "two heads are better than one." Creative solutions to many company problems emerge from a team approach that generates divergent possibilities. Generally, work addicts are not team players. Their urgent need to control makes it hard for them to cooperatively problem solve, and give and take in team situations. They believe their approach and style are the best answers and cannot entertain less perfect solutions. Spontaneity is diminished and creativity stifled when the narrow view of one addicted worker prevails.

The label "workhorse" refers to those who push themselves beyond human limitations. Pushing themselves to the maximum is routine behavior for abusive workers who grew up in homes where normal was undefined. Janet Woititz sampled 100 adult children of alcoholics and found that 87 percent had chosen stressful occupations. She concluded that adult children are drawn to stressful jobs without the tools to manage stress. Overwork and added stress help work addicts dilute their attention to personal needs. Overworking is a part of their general pattern of overdoing and overcompensating for poor self-worth from early dysfunctional upbringing. Work addicts can be difficult to work with because they create high-stress situations. Refusal or inability to delegate tasks, taking short cuts to speed up the company's process and rushing against unrealistic deadlines inevitably lower the quality of work production.

Addicted workers show the side effects of irritability and impatience with co-workers who may not produce fast enough. Flared tempers and angry outbursts become the norm. Disharmony prevails and group morale nose-dives, thwarting company effectiveness. As work abusers try to squeeze more work into less time, eventual burnout occurs for them and those under their supervision. An admitted work addict who supervises staff for a national broadcasting company told me that since he took his supervisory position, he has fast forwarded the pace of work in the office. He pushes his staff to get everything out of them that he can. And he must constantly monitor them for burnout. When the signs of stress appear, he orders them to slow down, go on a break or take a short vacation.

Work addicts can place themselves and others in danger when employed in certain hazardous jobs. Rushing through a job that requires manual dexterity with tools, machinery or heavy equipment can cause physical injury as well as damaged goods. Other occupations, such as airline pilots and brain surgeons — where patience, precision and clear thinking are paramount — do not lend themselves to the abusive worker's style of being mentally preoccupied with the next sequence of work requirements. When fatigue and stress escalate, the likelihood of accidents and errors also increases. Thus, many work addicts are less efficient than co-workers who put in fewer hours planning and working toward a job goal. Eventually the amount of effort addicted workers put into their jobs becomes disproportionate to the effectiveness of their work. As they continue to overinvest in their jobs, stress and burnout grow, and work efficiency declines.

Accompanying Addictions

Patterns of work abuse often include the use of other drugs, such as caffeine and cigarettes, to keep the body going and the momentum in supercharged careers. Stronger drugs, such as alcohol and marijuana, are also used in tandem with excessive work to relax and bring relief from accompanying withdrawal symptoms. An addicted worker for a major corporate sales force confessed how he used drugs as a crutch to help him balance a work day:

> I go home at night, frequently uptight and wound up about everything. I want to quit, to stop working. I'm home now — let's leave it behind. I'll pick it up tomorrow morning when I get to work. My release is to have a drink and mellow out a little bit.
>
> I don't see mine as an addiction yet, but I see that it could be if I continue to allow the stress to get to me. I could see myself getting home and having two or three drinks to completely forget and unwind.

A long-standing body of research has linked work addiction to the release of adrenalin in the body. Many of my respondents described a rush or surge of energy pumping through their veins. Several even identified the euphoria they felt from work excitement as an "adrenalin high." Adrenalin is a hormone, produced by the body in times of stress, that has a similar effect as amphetamines or "speed." Some researchers believe work addicts unconsciously put themselves under stressful situations to get the body to pump such a fix. Addicted to adrenalin, work addicts require larger doses to maintain the high that they create by putting themselves and those around them under stress. Adrenalin addiction, in effect, creates addictions to crises so that the body will produce the hormone, and work addicts will get their drug. On the job work addicts' managerial style is to re-create an uproar that they must resolve. Crises, which require the body's adrenalin flow, are routinely manufactured and doused. Another way they create stress is by driving themselves and pushing others to finish designated assignments within unrealistic deadlines. While work addicts get high, co-workers and subordinates experience many of the same emotions as children of alcoholics, notably unpredictability, confusion and frustration.

The Work Addict As "Boss"

Attempts to change and control other people lead many work addicts into management positions. Their poor communication skills, inability to express feelings and lack of sensitivity to employees usually make them ineffective managers. An employee criticized her work-addicted boss when he asked her what she thought about his management skills:

> You really want to know an honest answer, I'll tell you. I've come to him with something very crucial. He didn't really have time, but he worked me into his schedule. The whole time he was talking to me he was signing vouchers, answering the phone and hanging it up again. Then, he says, "Yeah, yeah tell me more." I felt like I never have his attention. He doesn't listen to anything I say. I don't do that to people. I come around from my desk and sit in front of them and really listen to what they have to say.

Work abusive supervisors and managers push their employees into their same addicted work patterns, even when it goes against the grain of the subordinates' natural work pace. Margaret, a nurse practitioner, shook her head in disbelief as she told of the unreasonable demands that her supervisor makes on the staff. The supervisor instructed Margaret to be prepared for an 11:30 p.m. phone call from another nurse who works the same job on the second shift. The late shift nurse did not know how to use a particular machine, so Margaret would have to teach her by phone and miss her regular

10:00 bedtime. Margaret pointed out that she had put in a stressful full day, was not being paid for the requested late-night work and had to report back on duty at 7:00 the next morning. "Don't you think that's an unreasonable request?" Margaret questioned her supervisor three different times.

"No, I don't," replied her supervisor, a compulsive overworker and adult child of an alcoholic, "I don't think it's unreasonable at all."

Cleveland, who works for a major corporation, told me about his manager's addictive work habits, which included making unreasonable demands and the inability to delegate:

> We had an opportunity to do a presentation for a quarter-million-dollar bid at an engineering school. I found out about the deal, went to my manager and told him we need to go for this, showing him my outline. He got on the phone, started calling the potential clients, got everything hyped-up and essentially took over my job. He came back to us and said that we were behind the eight ball here and that the other vendors were six to eight weeks ahead of us. He started saying that we had to get this much done, and we had to get it done within a week. He started throwing together a time line that was completely unrealistic if we were going to do a good presentation. In an attempt to slow him down, I told him to leave it alone and let me take it, and he agreed to do that. But as we started to develop the presentation, we started getting more messages like, "Have you thought of this?" "How's this going?" "Are you bringing other parties within and outside the company into the presentation?" He even called some outside sources and invited them to take part in the presentation, after I had already booked their competitors. He had to run the show, making us lose the whole deal!

When hiring personnel, some work-addicted bosses clone their employees in the perfectionistic images of themselves, as the interviewing practices of one work-addicted employer illustrates:

I cross every 'i' and dot every 't'. I try to head problems off at the pass by finding people like me to hire. When I'm interviewing, I pick up on people and say, "Hey, they're my kind of person." Until recently, I have not made any mistakes in picking out that trait in my personnel. Staff who were laid back, or couldn't buy into the loyalty and hard work eventually left. I look for enthusiasm, loyalty, a sense of commitment, and a desire to do the job and do it well.

The work-addicted boss is overcritical, overdemanding and unable to tolerate mistakes from subordinates. Employees get very little positive feedback for their work efforts that rarely are good enough to match the boss's expectations. No matter how hard they try to please, nothing is ever good enough to satisfy the abusive worker's perfectionist standards. The work addict's mood can swing from high to low in a work day or work week. Working for a supervisor, manager or foreman who experiences the adrenalin highs and irritable and restless withdrawals can be formidable. Some corporate workers have described the mood swings of corporate bosses as a Jekyll/Hyde personality. Employees are never sure what to say or do. They waste enormous amounts of energy trying to second-guess their employers. They suffer tension, poor self-esteem and loss of control. In effect, work-addicted managers carry their own family dysfunction into the workplace and re-create it in their relationships with employees. The work force is in effect a work family. In that "family" the bosses function as "parents" and subordinates as "children." The dynamics, then, in an addicted work family are similar to those that are created in true alcoholic households. Betrayal, deception, lies and mixed messages are some of the interactions that occur between work-addicted employers and their employees.

As the moods of the boss swing from high to low, employees try to appease their superior's desires by swinging back and forth as well. Addicted managers are notorious for making and breaking promises because unrealistic time frames cannot be achieved. So a new plan is substituted. The work climate is unpredictable and inconsistent, and morale is low — similar to the climate in alcoholic homes. Fear and insecurity are normal reactions for employees in unpredictable job positions. Workers become frustrated trying to match their behaviors with the boss's dictates.

Many problems befall employees as a result of the stresses and strains of their work-addicted environments. Emotions run the gamut from fear, anger, confusion, guilt and embarrassment to sadness and depression at not being able to measure up to the rules of the game. Employees do not know what normal is because rules or policies change periodically. In order to cope, subordinates guess at what their bosses want and often find themselves making stabs in the dark. Having a work-addicted employer for a prolonged time can lead to severe psychological damage to employees. Emotionally battered and bruised, many workers limp through their careers. Poor self-esteem, lack of control over their careers, poor coping skills and problems in interpersonal relationships all result in an attempt to meet dysfunctional demands from the powers that be. Work output that ordinarily goes into quality production is instead consumed by workers covering their tracks, lying and engaging in deceptive practices.

The true case of Stephanie illustrates how this cycle of interaction works. Stephanie's addictive work habits as district sales manager for a major computer sales corporation have made it so unbearable for one of her sales representatives, Alec, that he has devised his own coping strategies to survive. At 47, Stephanie gets up and goes to work by 7:30 a.m. and doesn't get home until eight or nine o'clock. She generally works at home for another couple of hours before she goes to bed. Frustrated at her work abuse, Stephanie's husband took a job traveling because his interests and needs were not being met in their relationship. Her obsession and constant driving within her profession leave no time for family life, and her social life includes only people within the company.

According to Alec, age 27, who works under Stephanie, she will not leave the sales representatives alone to do their jobs. Instead, she is burning herself out trying to keep her hands in everything they do. She spends most of her time trying to work their accounts rather than managing them. She cannot delegate, let it go and wait until a task is accomplished. She has to be intimately involved while the task is completed.

Alec also observes that work is everything to Stephanie. There is nothing else in her life but work. Her business associates have never known her to take a day off without her leaving one of them an electronic message. Most of her employees are frustrated. They are constantly beat up by her to get things done in a timely manner. Alec complains that she's always breathing down his neck by telephone and electronic messages. She's constantly concerned that things go like she wants them to go. She's too much of a perfectionist and afraid that nobody's going to do the job as well as she would do it if she were there. So she keeps her hands in everything.

Alec says that the morale of the sales reps is rock bottom. The sales team doesn't function as a real "team." Not only is teamwork broken down, but their spirits are shattered: "It's tough for me to turn a task over to somebody and feel like it's going to get accomplished as I have outlined it and discussed it with that person for fear that she's going to come around and make changes. This happens constantly."

The sales force is constantly frustrated that they are either not accomplishing enough in a time frame to satisfy Stephanie's desires, or that they cannot get done what they must accomplish because she keeps throwing other ideas at them that they consider to be insignificant. Alec also notes that the staff's frustration levels rise and fall in response to Stephanie's unpredictable behaviors.

Alec describes some of her erratic moods and the effects those moods have on the sales force:

We're ending our year right now; we're talking about splitting my territory and putting a new rep in the southern part of the state. In a four-day period, over a weekend, she changed her mind six times by electronic messages. She kept calling and said here's the way we're going to do it. Then she'd call back and change. The sixth message said, "I think what we're going to do is have you turn the files over to this person. Well, no. We'll talk about it on Monday." The way I overcome that unpredictability is to give her the answer she wants to hear and then push on and do things the way I think they should be done. I'll say, "Oh yes! Sure, sure! great idea!" A lot of times my agreeing with whatever she says satisfies her desire to stay in touch in whatever I'm doing. If there's something of value in what she says, I'll accept it. If not, I ignore it. Once the task is accomplished, there's no question about how it was accomplished. So I avoid a lot of conflict and frustration on my part by lying and pacifying her. I overcompensate for what she does or I ignore her phone calls for a couple of days and try to sidetrack her.

Some of my fellow workers try to respond to everything she wants, and they're getting as crazy as she is, just constantly working. If you're buried in the middle of two or three things and she starts this routine, I've seen people come into the office with bloodshot eyes, completely drained. They look as if they haven't slept in three or four days. It's really rough.

We always know the reaction we're going to get out of her. She's going to give the immediate response that pops in her head. It's sometimes Jekyll and Hyde because it's tough to read which way she'll go immediately. She's constantly flying off the handle and jumping down people's throats, venting frustrations of her own. If you're under the pile (that is, you've got too much to do and you're really suffering), she helps you build up a frustration level and get buried in your pile of work. Then, she will pounce on you too.

When she notices we're covered up with things to do, she starts harping on what we're doing and picking on a selected victim. Everybody always knows when they get on her list. She starts looking over our shoulders. She sees us getting buried, not responding like she would, then she jumps us. Rather than helping take the load off, she puts more stress on us.

Dysfunctional Work Roles

The survival roles of subordinates who work under tyrannical managerial styles take identical forms that children acquire in addicted families. The interworkings of the company department are dependent on each employee who functions as an interdependent part of the overall departmental system. As the department works together to run smoothly, any change in one part of the department will result in automatic changes in other parts. The department will always try to keep itself on an even keel. As the head of the department gets out of kilter with her work addiction, all members of the department are thrown off balance, and shift their behaviors to survive and to accommodate the unbalance. As Stephanie's managerial style became more dysfunctional, for example, Alec and his co-workers shifted from their ordinary way of response to dysfunctional behaviors, such as deception and lies. Thus, many of the same interactive patterns of addicted families have been re-created in the workplace.

As work addiction progresses, the whole department becomes progressively sicker too. Everything revolves around the addicted boss whose behavior dictates how subordinates interact inside and outside the work force. Each worker adapts to the boss's behavior by developing behaviors that cause the least amount of personal stress. Workers adapt roles of superiority (company hero), aggression (company rebel), withdrawal (lost worker) and wit (company clown) in response to work-addicted employers. These roles parallel those that Sharon

Wegscheider identified among children in dysfunctional or addicted families, namely the family hero, scapegoat, lost child and mascot.

The organization itself is the *chief enabler* because it stresses continued productivity at any cost. As the boss becomes progressively more addicted, the higher-ups toss accolades that encourage him to keep up the momentum.

There is often one worker in the department, usually one with the most seniority, who emerges as the *company hero*. This role brings harmony and stability to the company. Heroes try to protect colleagues from the boss's abusive managerial style. They may jump in to help out a co-worker who is overloaded, organize a group to rebut unrealistic deadlines or even stand up against the boss to speak out the frustrations of the work family. Lech Walesa, organizer of Solidarity, is a work hero for millions of people in Poland, and Cesar Chavez fills that role for the United Farm Workers of America.

Some employees adopt the role of *company rebel* in the work world to cope with unreasonable job demands. Company rebels are the disruptive colleague in the department. They can never seem to do anything right and constantly fail because of self-sabotage. Rather than following company policy, they take short cuts, undermine the boss's authority, or engage in bitter squabbles with employers and co-workers. Rebels internalize company frustrations by getting into trouble on the job. They may take money from the business, telling themselves, "This company doesn't care about us anyway," or "I figure they owe me a few extra dollars with all I've done for them and the low salary they pay me." Rebels may also act out their frustrations by physically assaulting or verbally abusing the boss or co-workers. They may throw a fit and destroy company equipment or property. Or their ire may take the form of more verbal aggression.

A professor in a College of Education, for instance, aggressively tried to undermine the dean of his college in almost every academic policy that was put forward. The verbally abusive faculty member even went so far as to call a meeting of all college-wide faculty members to protest, point by point, the items on the dean's agenda. The professor's unruly and unprofessional behavior eventually estranged colleagues who did not wish to be associated with his aggressive style of attack. Of course, rebels do not last long. Typically, they would be fired or referred for counseling or both.

There are a few employees who become *lost workers* and turn their feelings inward. They are neither troublemakers nor leaders. They adapt to the departmental dysfunction by following directions and accepting whatever comes their way, no matter how inconsistent or contradictory. They clam up and withdraw from co-workers, remaining quietly in the background and trying to behave as they are expected. They adjust because they do not make an emotional investment in their jobs. If they are not emotionally involved, then the chaos and job stress doesn't affect them as badly. At their first opportunity, they abandon ship by finding employment elsewhere, perhaps never voicing their frustration and dissatisfaction.

The fourth role in the company is that of *company clown*. Company clowns cover up their anguish and frustration by generally lightening the department's problems by diversion through humor and fun. They are always full of wisecracks and jokes to entertain co-workers. They make light of the boss's demands and try to keep the tone upbeat, everybody happy and nothing too serious. Although they are the life of the party, underneath their jovial nature clowns have difficulty handling stress. They are sad, afraid, insecure and alone. Their role as stand-up comic keeps them out of serious work commitments, and employers might wonder if they take their work seriously enough to make important decisions or to handle responsibilities.

The four roles of superiority (company hero), aggression (company rebel), withdrawal (lost worker) and wit (company clown) are workers' responses to work-addicted employers. Company heads who have internalized dysfunctional behaviors from their families transfer them into the workplace, re-creating them in a new and dysfunctional departmental system that filters down to everyone in the organization. Thus, the disease of addiction is perpetuated and spreads throughout the entire business organization.

Counterproductivity And Work Addiction

Work is fundamental to the basis of our society. The Puritan work ethic has always been valued in this country. Hard work has been linked to good, clean living as an antidote to sin and evil. There has never been anything wrong with someone who worked too hard. If their marriages crumbled and kids got into trouble, hard workers were exonerated and other family members swiftly accused: "They have always worked so hard for their families, and that's the thanks they get."

Our society has rewarded work addiction since it was founded. Still today addictive work is prized by corporate America despite the fact that, when converted to dollars and cents, work addiction is clearly counterproductive. Big business promotes the all-or-none thinking of adult children of alcoholics by suggesting that you give it all you've got or you're out. There is no in between. But addictive work practices actually circumvent economic growth and prosperity. The biggest cost factors are absenteeism, tardiness and drops in morale because of stress and burnout.

One work addict put it this way:

> Work reinforces our addictions. We are rewarded for killing ourselves. My boss has too much to do. He has more to do than it is possible for him to do. So do I. I work two jobs. They want your body and soul. When everybody is carrying that much of a burden, management-wise, you begin to hear people saying a lot of

negatives. As that happens, it starts eroding at the base of the company of your middle management. Then, if middle management is negative, it filters on down to the work force, and you lose the whole thing.

Stress and burnout lead to health problems, which in turn lead to absenteeism, tardiness and reduced employee productivity. Ultimately, businesses lose money because of abusive work habits. Work addicts have poor nutrition since they eat on the run and do not always get proper exercise because the time it takes interferes with work. These two factors combined cause illnesses, such as viruses and colds, as well as various psychosomatic disorders. Work productivity is also negatively affected when work addicts suffer from depression that lowers motivation and increases work absences. High blood pressure, heart disease, abdominal problems and a host of other illnesses also cost businesses money. Heart disease alone, which is linked to job stress, is responsible for an annual loss of 135 million workdays.

Premature deaths from heart disease and suicides — often stemming from organizational problems — contribute to a tragic loss of human potential in the work force. Overall estimates reveal that absenteeism, diminished productivity, medical expenses and related problems caused by stress and burnout cost the nation's employers $150 billion a year.

Work addiction promotes an atmosphere of on-the-job unhappiness, instability and insecurity. Companies that breed work addiction have a work force that is less cohesive, less organized, more conflict-ridden and less oriented toward creative pursuits. Their energies are consumed from trying to keep their sinking work ship afloat, and they spend a larger portion of time treading water than producing. Environments that are plagued by frequent quarreling, high stress, unrealistic employer demands and lack of concern for the health and psychological welfare of employees are ineffective competitors in the world of work. Abused by the organizational system, impending doom becomes the silent companion of the work force. Anxiety and lack of trust cause workers to wonder who will be next to "get the ax." The natural response to such unnatural dynamics is unnatural, dysfunctional behaviors. These unhealthy patterns pervade corporate America today, ultimately filter down to the rank and file of the nation's workers, and sabotage the quality of work productivity.

Recovery In The Workplace

In the past the corporate world believed that ranks of work-addicted employees would guarantee greater production. But in truth, corporations achieve more creative results and greater revenues from a more balanced work force. Salespersons who have achieved balance in their lives, for example, are more apt to attract potential clients than obsessed, high-pressured ones who are more likely to turn clients off and drive them away.

How can corporate America take all the problems of work addiction and convert them into dollars and cents? That is the question that is being asked more and more today. Many businesses are refusing to hire known work abusers. Finding cost-effective ways to balance work and other life responsibilities is now a major concern for employers in the United States. More employers are taking active steps to close the great divide between work and family responsibilities. Employee assistance programs have undertaken major new responsibilities for work and family-related issues, such as stresses and strains that occur on the job. And more bosses are telling employees, directly or indirectly, to slow down.

Stephanie's boss rejected a vacation card she had submitted to get vacation credits because she had left him electronic messages that same day. He told her, "You were not on vacation because you sent me a message, so take another day of vacation. Get away from the office and forget about work for a while."

Corporate America can help interrupt the disease of work addiction and still reap quality production and financial benefits. The following suggestions will help eradicate compulsive work patterns in the job market:

Raise The Employer's Awareness

Trained consultants can work closely with organizational personnel to brief them on the problems that many adult children of alcoholics transfer into their jobs. The dangers of work addiction and how to spot its symptoms in themselves and employees can also be addressed. A plan of action for interrupting the disease and improving the work climate can be adapted to the company's unique needs.

Conduct In-Service Workshops For Employee Assistance Program Personnel

More assertive efforts by Employee Assistance Programs (EAP) to recognize and treat work abuse as a legitimate form of addiction will give employees seeking help a bona fide support system. These programs can be instrumental in drawing attention to and promoting support for those who need it.

Raise The Employee's Awareness

Establishment of addiction awareness days in the company can be done with posters and special seminars featuring the many types of addictions that exist in families and in the work force. Information can be presented through outside speakers so that all workers learn about the effects of addictions and children of alcoholics in a nonthreatening way. The awareness days can serve as a springboard to establishing special groups for adult children of alcoholics and work addicts.

Encourage Special 12-Step Group Meetings

Such 12-Step groups as Al-Anon or Adult Children of Alcoholics can meet before or after work, or during lunch at designated places on the work site. It is important that corporate America see the denial hidden in recommendations from business consultants who eschew the need for a group founded on the principles of Alcoholics Anonymous. There are many special 12-Step groups for a variety of addictions: Alcoholics Anonymous, Overeaters Anonymous, Al-Anon, Adult Children of Alcoholics, Gamblers Anonymous, Narcotics Anonymous, Co-dependents Anonymous, Debtors Anonymous, Sexual Incest Anonymous and Sex Addicts Anonymous. There is even a 12-Step program for those suffering from the effects of upbringing in religious addiction. The fact that no special 12-Step program exists for work addicts attests to society's denial that work can be a true addiction. Compulsive workers need a 12-Step program of their own, such as Work Addicts Anonymous, so that they can effectively deal with their disease. By meeting together and talking about their problems, work addicts are less isolated, less ashamed and have a rich support system to draw on in the job setting. With minimum effort, business and industry can provide the opportunity for recovery to millions of workers.

Disseminate Information To Employees Through Available Avenues

Through avenues already available in the organization, companies can offer aerobics classes, meditation workshops, stress-reduction classes and exercise programs during work breaks. These can raise employee awareness of the signs of stress and burnout, and can show how to combat them. Special seminars on how to identify work addiction and how to interrupt it before it takes its toll could be presented. Community speakers can be engaged to talk about the 12-Step programs and their location in the community, and to familiarize employees with their usefulness. Company bulletin boards, newsletters and other publications are valuable dissemination resources on all these topics.

Start A Lending Library

A corner of a waiting area, health room, lounge or other underused area at the work site can house the collection in a minimal amount of space. Stock it with pamphlets, books, newsletters and magazines dealing with addictions, work abuse and adult children of alcoholics issues. Materials can be catalogued and checked out on a regular basis, using an honor system. Reading of these materials promotes knowledge, changes attitudes and reduces feelings of isolation.

Sponsor Company Celebrations

Work does not have to be serious all the time. The company that plays together stays together. Fun and light-heartedness relieve stress and make the work environment more enjoyable. Social times also unify employees and help them to function more cohesively by getting them acquainted on a more personal basis. Company picnics, reunions, retirement parties, holiday office parties and special birthday parties for co-workers are just a few examples of how business can blend work with play. And the emphasis on alcoholic beverages can be downplayed by serving nonalcoholic alternatives.

Explore New Ways To Balance Work With Other Areas Of Life

Hiring practices can be established to bring balanced employees on board who can build a work climate of security, satisfaction, creativity and productivity. Ways to restructure the work responsibilities of employees can be created so that they are encouraged to spend time on personal, home and social commitments. Some of the possibilities include: (1) *paternity leave*, which gives fathers opportunities to participate in childbirth and child rearing; (2) *flexitime*, which allows workers to complete a fixed number of hours per week, geared around their personal lives; (3) *job sharing*, which involves two people sharing one full-time job by arranging their work duties and schedules to meet employer needs; (4) *flexiplace*, which enables workers to perform their work duties at home, and is likely to become increasingly popular in the future as more computer links are made between offices and homes.

The removal of work addiction from the workplace can erase burnout and stress, health problems, poor communication and low morale. Employers, employees and consumers all benefit. It can save business and industry billions of dollars a year, provide a better work climate for employees and a better product for consumers.

Steps To Personal Recovery

The Nature Of Recovery From Work Addiction

I have mentioned all through this book that work addicts feel something is missing in their lives. They try to fill that void through working at their jobs and staying busy. Work is a substitute for the spiritual hunger that only recovery can satisfy. Although work addicts can and do recover, self-sabotage is their biggest threat because personal healing requires more work, the very thing that addicted persons are trying to overcome. Your natural inclination will be to approach recovery in the same way you approach work — to hurry up, cram it in your schedule and rush through it. Such an approach is self-defeating because recovery cannot be rushed.

Abusive work habits do not begin at age 21 or 30; they start in childhood and have a long history with a stronghold on your life. Don't expect to reverse the early patterns in one day, week or even a month. There is no such thing as a "quick fix" approach. My favorite poster is a breathtaking picture of the Grand Canyon that took nature centuries to carve. The caption says, "Things Take Time." Recovery from work addiction does not happen overnight either. It is a gradual process as is withdrawal from any addictive substance, and it takes commitment and time. Give yourself plenty of time for recovery to occur and give yourself credit for small gains you make. Rather than focusing on all that needs to be done, pat yourself on the back for the baby steps you make along the way. It takes time to change the patterns that took you 30 or 40 years to develop. This is an important reminder so that you won't become frustrated and sabotage your healing process. You will not see an immediate concrete product that you are accustomed to. However, if you stay with it, you eventually will start seeing results.

Recovery has already started if you are aware that you are addicted to work, and it will continue just as slowly and gradually as the addiction did when it got its foothold. Don't give up. Allow the process and approach it as an exciting new adventure that unfolds with each new day. There is a whole unexplored world waiting for you to experience.

The Balance Wheel Of Life

As recovering persons reorganize their lives to allow more space for growth, work becomes proportionate to life's other commitments. Achieving and maintaining balance is the goal of those who want to develop their full potential. Work addicts are thrown off balance because of the neglect of other areas in their lives. If you want to move forward on the road of recovery, your wheels have to be balanced. We function as harmonious and whole human beings when balance occurs in four major areas of life: healthy work, family, play and self areas. The self area includes attending to such personal needs as spiritual nurturance, nutrition and physical exercise. Family includes positive communication and communion with loved ones. Today's society has many family configurations so that "family" means many different things to different people. Your family can be a spouse; it can include both a spouse and children; it can include unmarried lovers who cohabitate, or adults who reside with older parents or siblings. The play arena extends our needs for social relationships with others outside the family. Healthy work habits include being effective and productive on the job, enjoying what we do for a living, working moderately and giving equal time to other areas of our lives.

Achieving this balance is sometimes a tightwire act. One way to view your life is to imagine it as a wheel made up of four spokes: *healthy work, family, play* and *self.* Each spoke is valued equally and gets equal attention if your wheel is to keep its shape. When one quadrant is unattended, the circle starts to deflate, loses its shape, and becomes unbalanced and lopsided. Nobody is perfectly balanced. But the closer you come, the fuller, more centered, and more alive you feel as a human being. And you will become a more self-contented person all the way **around.**

Taking time to develop a balance among all four areas of your life wheel will ensure more harmony within yourself, at home, at work and at play. The following inventory will help you find the area in which balance is lacking. Knowledge of where imbalance of life occurs will help you develop a recovery plan.

Life Inventory

There are four areas to this life inventory: **healthy work, family, play** and **self.** Using the rating scale of 1 *(never true)*, 2 *(seldom true)*, 3 *(often true)* and 4 *(always true)*, put the number that best fits you in the blank beside each statement. At the end of each area you will get your total score by adding the eight numbers in each area and putting the sum in the blank at the end of the area.

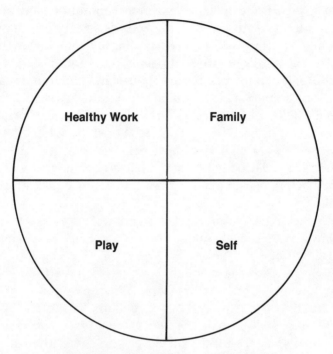

Figure 8.1. The Balance Wheel of Life

Area 1: Healthy Work

_____ 1. I have many interests outside my work duties.

_____ 2. I spend as much time after hours with family and friends as I do with co-workers.

_____ 3. I enjoy my work today as much as ever, and I am productive and effective at what I do.

_____ 4. I work overtime only on special occasions.

_____ 5. I am able to leave my work at the workplace.

_____ 6. I am good at organizing and pacing my work time so that it doesn't interfere with other commitments.

_____ 7. I work moderately, pace myself, and confine my job to regular working hours.

_____ 8. I spend an equal amount of time relaxing and socializing with friends as I do working.

_____ **Total Work Score**

Area 2: Family

_____ 1. I communicate well with the members of my family.

_____ 2. I take an active interest in the lives of my other family members.

_____ 3. My family spends quality time together.

_____ 4. My family plays together and takes family outings regularly.

_____ 5. I participate actively in family celebrations, traditions and rituals.

_____ 6. I have good interpersonal relationships with other family members.

_____ 7. I enjoy spending time with my family.

_____ 8. My family and work life are in harmony with each other.

_____ **Total Family Score**

Area 3: Play

_____ 1. I socialize with friends who are not co-workers.

_____ 2. I enjoy social gatherings.

_____ 3. I like to unwind with friends.

_____ 4. I go out socially with friends.

_____ 5. My social life and work life are in harmony with each other.

_____ 6. I enjoy inviting friends to my house for dinner.

_____ 7. I like to play and have fun with others.

_____ 8. It feels good to laugh, have a fun time and get my mind off work.

_____ **Total Play Score**

Area 4: Self

_____ 1. I plan time each day just for me to do whatever I want to do.

_____ 2. For fun I have a hobby or recreation that I enjoy.

_____ 3. I take time out each week for my spiritual development, either church or synagogue, inspirational readings, meditation or a 12-Step program.

_____ 4. I eat nutritional, well balanced meals.

_____ 5. I make sure I get adequate rest.

_____ 6. I take physical exercise daily.

_____ 7. I send myself positive mental messages and try to look for the best in myself.

_____ 8. I make sure I get my personal needs met.

_____ **Total Self Score**

Scoring

Using the Balance Wheel of Life that follows, put an "X" on the number in each area that corresponds with your total score. Draw a line from that number to the center of the wheel. Then darken the entire area of the circle from your total score back to the number "8." For example, if your **total self score** is 16, put an X over the number 16 in the **self** area of the wheel. Draw a line from 16 to the center of the circle; darken that area from the center outward, and between 8 and 16. Repeat these steps for all four areas of the wheel. That part of the wheel that has the biggest shaded area is the area in which you are most balanced. The part that is less complete is the area of your life that needs attention.

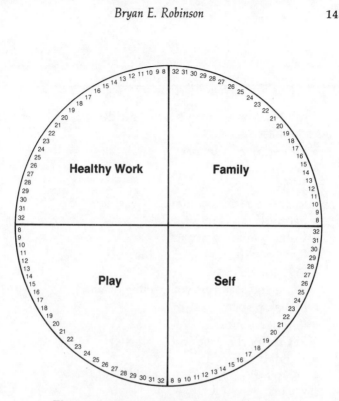

Figure 8.2. Your Balance Wheel of Life

Balancing Work Life

Work abusers are likely to be deflated in all four self-areas of their lives. Although work is their main focus, healthy work habits are usually missing from their lives. Balance in the work area requires slowing down the work pace, learning to relax and working in moderation.

Slow Down Your Work Pace

Make a conscious effort to slow down the pulse and rhythm of your daily life. Set aside a period of time to deliberately eat slower, talk slower, walk slower and drive slower. Learn to say no when you are already overcommitted and have a choice of accepting or rejecting a work request. Delegate work to those who

Steps To Personal Recovery

The following steps will guide you toward personal recovery:
- Slow down your pace.
- Learn to relax.
- Work in moderation.
- Improve family climate.
- Strengthen family ties.
- Celebrate life's rituals.
- Get back in the social swing.
- Live in the now.
- Build social networks outside of work.
- Develop social pastimes.
- Pamper yourself.
- Eat properly, rest and exercise.
- Validate yourself.
- Mourn the loss of your childhood.
- Seek spiritual healing.
- Attend a 12-Step program.
- Apply the 12 Steps of AA.

can effectively accomplish the task. Avoid putting yourself under unrealistic deadlines or putting self-imposed time limits on important things that must get done. Give yourself extra time to get to where you need to go or to do whatever you need to complete. Deliberately build time cushions into your schedule. One of the things I did was to schedule my appointments 30 minutes apart rather than 15 minutes apart. That gave me a chance to catch my breath, go to the restroom or just stretch and have a casual conversation with a colleague or friend.

In addition, put important decisions on the back burner of your mind, rather than acting hastily, and think them through before taking action. You will find that you make wiser decisions and save time in the long run because you do not leave a thoughtless mess to clean up behind you. Interrupt your work day with periodic breathers in between unusually long or complicated work sessions or meetings. Take time to stretch, get a soft drink or take a walk with a friend.

Learn To Relax

There are many ways to relax. Eliminate the stress that work creates by practicing stress-relief exercises. Mind relaxation techniques are very important for those who work in busy jobs. Yoga, meditation, massage and relaxation exercises are ways to unwind, and come down from "work highs." Take a breather from work, close your office door or, if you don't have an office, find a quiet space where you can be alone. Close your eyes and relieve tension by practicing relaxation exercises. Access to soft music will promote relaxation as you meditate or lead yourself through guided imagery. Lack of on-the-job facilities might require that you practice these tension reduction exercises at home in the mornings or after work.

Chapter 9 contains suggested readings that provide a series of stress reduction activities. As a result of these activities, you will feel more refreshed, think more clearly, and perform more efficiently and creatively on your job.

Work In Moderation

Some work addicts fluctuate between highs and lows with their work-related activities. They may swing from frantic productivity to total inertia. But rarely do work addicts confine their work to regular working hours. Most addictions require 100 percent abstinence. But work abuse must be managed with balance because some degree of work is necessary for survival. Thus, work moderation is the goal for the recovering addict. Keep an even keel by abstaining from excessive work. Try to establish a more steady work schedule with regular hours rather than working all the time or binging for weeks at a time. When possible, try to confine your working hours to eight hours a day, five days a week.

Go against the habit of self-imposing strict, unrealistic deadlines and spread them out over a longer period of time. Although this schedule may not fit your line of work, try to tailor moderation around your unique situation. Individuals must define their own work moderation because every job is different and time requirements, job parameters and job commitments vary. As you achieve work moderation, you'll see the pendulum start to swing to the center, as you begin to balance your work activities with the rest of your life.

Balancing Family Life

Practically all work addicts have neglected their families and find during recovery that they need to put a lot more energy into family life. This is accomplished by improving family climate, rebuilding shaky relationships and catching up on family events that they have missed.

Improve Family Climate

Close scrutiny of existing family climate is important. Family climate refers to the temperament of the family on a daily basis and can range from stormy to sunny. By eliminating undue stress and tension where possible, the family functions more smoothly and happily. Try to focus on the positive things family members do rather than harping on the negative. Everybody has bad days, but try not to come home in foul moods or unload your anger or frustration on other family members. Instead, try dealing with work problems before coming home or taking a few minutes to yourself when you get home to unwind and set a pleasant tone for family evenings.

Strengthen Family Ties

Strong families view their lives together and the energy required to maintain healthy family ties as a privilege and challenge — not as obligation or struggle. One of the best ways to strengthen family bonds is to plan evenings together as a family. Preparing meals together and having pleasant mealtime conversations (without television) give families a chance for healthy communication. Take a genuine and active interest in your family's life. Listen to what they have to say. Find out what they have been up to during the week.

If you have children, plan times to give them special, undivided attention. Save newspaper reading until they are asleep. Plan time with youngsters by helping them with homework, playing board games, scheduling weekday or weekend family outings, or conducting family projects. Examples include:

- Make a scrapbook of your family or town history.
- Trace the best route for your summer vacation.
- Create new family recipes.
- Make a family garden.
- Design family Christmas cards.
- Write songs or poetry.
- Design a family emblem.
- Take nature walks to collect leaves, feathers, etc.

Start the morning off on a positive note with pleasant words and calm routines. Limit the amount of work you bring home in the evenings and on weekends. Save some of that time for special moments with your most precious resources, those that love you.

Celebrate The Rituals In Your Life

Rituals, such as family celebrations, family traditions and patterned family interactions, are the glue that cement the family fabric together, and give it meaning and an identity of its own. Researchers Steven Wolin and Linda Bennett found that when families stick together by celebrating family meals, birthdays, holidays, graduations, anniversaries, reunions and so forth, the disease of addiction is less likely to be transmitted to the children. It is essential for work addicts to take time out to acknowledge rituals, the passage of time or the markers on the road of life. They help us appreciate the here and now — "what is" rather than "what will be." Some compulsive workers speed through important rituals, one day waking up and saying, "Oh, is she married already?" or "Is old Mrs. Smith still living?" Many of them do not remember their own anniversaries or they work through important holidays.

Take the time to recognize and reward yourself for your accomplishments, and those of your family and loved ones. Celebrate the rituals in your life with vigor and enthusiasm. Work addicts sometimes fool themselves by saying, "If I just take three or four more hours, I can get finished. There will always be another Christmas or birthday." But the truth is that there will never be another one just like the one you miss. There will be another year or another place, perhaps, but it will never be the same. Many nonrecovering work abusers feel deeply guilty looking back over the years and realizing they missed the experience of their kids growing up: Tommy's first birthday, Susie's graduation from high school and Joey's wedding day. And they have nothing to show for the missed memories. No amount of work can ever replace these important milestones in life; once they are missed, they are gone forever.

Balancing Play Life

Work addicts' best friend is work. They have few friends or acquaintances and few invitations to social functions. Getting back into the social swing of things is difficult when you have been socially isolated for so long. Play needs refer to the satisfaction of social needs and can include lots of activities, such as parties, hobbies, sports, reunions, church or synagogue fellowship, social clubs or community involvement.

Get Back Into The Social Swing

The best way to start is with a small dinner party of your own at home. That way you are on your own turf, and you can invite as many or as few people as you feel comfortable. An additional safety net is to renew old acquaintances with people for whom you genuinely care but with whom you have lost touch. To break any uneasiness, let it be a dinner party in which everyone participates in the leisurely preparation of the meal. Make the mealtime itself an evening's entertainment with fun, laughter and interesting conversation. You do not need to become a social butterfly to round out your Balance Wheel of Life, but some social interaction is important to steer you away from work, as well as to satisfy your basic human needs as a social being. Once you begin to feel comfortable in small and large groups, venture out and meet new people from whom you can grow and to whom you can reciprocate that growth.

Live In The Now

Pay attention to the people you are with at the moment, focus on the present and work on your relationships by putting time and energy into them. Show a genuine interest in those you spend time with as human beings. Really listen to what they have to say. Begin living for today and resist your mind's attempts to preoccupy you with tomorrow or next week. Focus on the beauty of a sunset, a painting, a bouquet of flowers. Take time to enjoy long walks and heart-to-heart talks with business associates, friends or family whom you have neglected.

Rediscover things in your world that you take for granted or ignore. Look at people and things around you as if you are seeing and enjoying them for the first time. Take time to look at what is on your office wall, to smell the flowers on someone's desk, to see the color of a blouse or jacket a colleague is wearing, the threads of the carpet in your house or the architecture of the houses in your neighborhood. Look into the eyes of a loved one or a friend and think about what you see there. Eat your meals more slowly and more deliberately. Think about the ingredients in what you are eating and savor the taste of every morsel. You will taste your food in a different way; for example, rather than just tasting tuna salad, you discover the wonderful flavor of celery, pickles, tuna and green lettuce. This technique does wonders for broadening your horizons, helping focus on the now and improving digestion.

Build Social Networks Outside Of Work

Join a social club or civic group that does not include work colleagues. This outside link to new friends can stimulate and expand your own interests and talents beyond your daily work role. Consider the following:

- Aerobic class
- Tennis or golf lessons
- Art class
- Church committee
- Cooking class
- Reading club
- Gardening club
- Running club
- Photography club

Develop Social Pastimes

Kate told me:

> I don't have any hobbies. I've done all kinds of causes and committees, changing the laws here and there, and picking up the cross and carrying it with a lot of things. But I don't paint, sew, draw, bowl or sing. I'm not very sportsy. When I'm not in my office, I read, usually professional journals and self-help books. I haven't read any fiction in 15 years.

Everyone can find some type of hobby that takes them outside the work domain and gets them into human interactions. Making space for an enjoyable pastime will help you put and keep your life on even keel. Find a hobby, recreation or creative outlet that allows your self-expression. Above all, give yourself credit for the expression of creative ideas and thoughts rather than depending on positive reactions from others. Hobbies, recreation and leisure provide outlets for an array of pent-up emotions — anger, sadness, fear, embarrass-ment, rage and loneliness — and also give you a sense of control over your life.

My favorite pastimes are tennis, creative writing and exercise. I sometimes release my playful child through street skating, which I do not recommend for everyone because of the obvious safety hazards. I even have tried my hand at acting as you read in the Introduction to the book.

The pastime you choose can be something you are *not* perfect at, and it does not have to culminate in a tangible product. The activity can give you sheer enjoyment from the process of self-involvement. It can be a group activity, such as an art class, or it can be an individual activity that you can share with others. Try your hand at painting, keeping a journal, handbuilding with clay, playing a musical instrument, gardening, cooking, writing creatively, composing poetry, woodworking or remodeling, and becoming involved in any of the art forms, organized sports or leisure activities that feel right for you. There is no prescribed way to select. Just base your choice on what you would enjoy, and what best suits your interests and schedule.

Balancing The Self

Since work abuse leads to self-neglect, it comes as no surprise that the personal area of the Balance Wheel of

Life is often the most deflated for work addicts. It is essential that you take some time in recovery to attend to your needs for a change. Personal and undivided attention to your physical, mental, nutritional, health, emotional and spiritual needs is crucial for your recovery. As you become more balanced in the other areas, you begin a metamorphosis of becoming a new person. You will always need structured personal and private time to stay acquainted with the new self that emerges during this transformation.

Pamper Yourself

Indulge yourself. Set aside a block of time, starting with one hour. Get reacquainted with the new person you are becoming. Look in the mirror. Groom yourself. Soak in a long, warm bath; relax by a fire or on a cool screened porch; or listen to soft music. Whatever you decide to do, you must deliberately block all work-related thoughts as they try to enter your mind. This hour is for you to do whatever you want. But you must have the cooperation of both your body and mind to get the benefits. You may feel boredom or restlessness the first time you try it, but don't give up.

You will actually experience some withdrawal from work, resulting in more boredom and restlessness. Recognize the symptoms and experience them. You are not used to paying this much attention to yourself, so your mind and body will naturally resist at first. Withdrawal symptoms will eventually disappear if you do this often and long enough.

Increase the amount of time you pamper yourself from one hour a week to one hour every day until you have built it into your regular schedule. Eventually you can work toward a full day of pampering and ultimately to a week. Before you know it, you will be able to take week-long vacations without work. But remember to take it gradually and one step at a time.

Eat Properly, Rest And Exercise

To put your mind and body in optimal shape, as well as to maximize recovery, eat right, get ample rest and exercise. Again, balance is the key. Eat balanced, nutritional meals instead of junk food. Eat three meals a day rather than one or two. Avoid eating while working, mealtime in front of the television and snacking between meals. Make meals a special time where nothing else happens but healthy communication with loved ones. Have an occasional candlelight dinner with fresh flowers.

Build rest and exercise into your schedule, and they will actually improve work effectiveness. Similar to an athlete primed for a race, you will be more physically and mentally fit. You will naturally think and create better when you are rested and have exercised. Rest and exercise will also cut down on health problems, such as headaches and stomachaches, that interfere with work quality. They will reduce more serious problems such as heart attacks and strokes.

Try building in a minimum of 30 minutes of exercise a day. You may need to consult a physician to establish the specifics of your exercise regimen, depending upon your health and age. But the activity you choose should match your health and physical capacity, as well as your interests. Be sure to do something you enjoy or at least pick the one you like most from your options.

I used to run three or four miles a day but had to give it up because of a back injury. Now I am an avid tennis player. I have also built into my work schedule between 30 and 90 minutes of low-impact aerobics and weight lifting each day. This fits my schedule best because the YMCA is only one minute from my house and the facility offers a wide variety of exercise options from which to choose. I have been religious with my exercise schedule for over two years. It keeps down my weight, stress level and cholesterol (which is exceptionally high) and keeps up my energy, lucidness and zest for life.

Walking, bicycling, organized sports, swimming and dancing are examples of other forms of exercise that can be matched to individual interests and situations.

Validate Yourself

Keep a bulletin board with all the validating letters, notes, gifts and sayings that people send you. Look at them often to remind yourself that others see you as a wonderful human being, despite the fact that you have to be constantly reminded of it.

I keep a bulletin board with personal reminders on it in my kitchen and I often put messages to myself on the bathroom mirror. In the morning I look myself straight in the eye and say the message, "You are looking at an incredibly wonderful human being!" or "You are looking at the only person in the world who can stand in the way of your happiness."

These sayings are by no means self-centered because they are true — not just of me, but of all of us who have been designed that way by nature. More than just repeating the phrase, which may be mechanical at first, you must really feel the message inside; this will come with time and lots of patience. As the old saying goes, the only difference between a stumbling block and stepping stones is how you use them. Validation is generated when we send ourselves balanced messages.

The following ten messages show the difference between balanced and unbalanced messages:

Unbalanced Messages	Balanced Messages
"I want to be loved by everyone."	"It would be nice to be loved by everyone, but that is unrealistic. My worth doesn't depend on everyone liking me."
"I must be thoroughly competent in all tasks that I undertake."	"Trying to be outstanding even in one task is very difficult. Achieve-

	"ments do not determine my worth."
"Other people upset me."	"I let other people upset me."
"My unhappiness is usually caused by events and people over which I have no control."	"I can control many of the things that happen to me by asserting my needs and opinions."
"I am responsible for the happiness of my family."	"I am responsible for my behavior and happiness, others are responsible for their behavior and happiness."
"I avoid problems hoping that they will go away."	"Facing problems early on results in less hassle and is more rewarding."
"I can't help the way I am."	"It is up to me to change the things I can that get me in trouble."
"My way is the best way."	"There are many ways to get something done. Mine is only one way. I am willing to listen and negotiate."
"Things have to be perfect for me to be happy."	"Life is uncertain, and people, myself included, are not perfect."
"My destiny is set."	"Anything is possible. I take responsibility for my future."

Mourn The Loss Of Your Childhood

The work addicts' defenses are strong. The hurt and pain from their dysfunctional childhoods are buried under piles of ledgers, reports and computer printouts.

Underneath and deep within each work addict's heart is a wounded child whose needs have been neglected from the focus on the external work world. It is difficult for the work abuser to reach those inner feelings. The barriers that prevent work abusers from being intimate, developing close relationships and feeling, in general, are hard for counselors and loved ones to penetrate. They may have few or no friends and immerse themselves in their jobs to fulfill relationship needs.

Work abusers become resentful and bitter adults whose childhoods have passed them. Mourning the loss of childhood rids work addicts of their uptight, rigid and inflexible masks. Missing out on a magical, joyful and carefree childhood is good reason to mourn. This grieving may take the form of anger at your inability to relive an important part of life that has passed you by, or it may emerge through sadness as you would mourn the loss of a loved one through death or divorce. Once mourning has occurred, the recovering person can get in touch with the inner playful child. Learn to play, relax and have fun. Welcome laughter, light-heartedness, and funny stories and jokes during the day. As Rokelle Lerner says, "Connecting the head and the heart through humor and play can be just as healing as the work we do with anger, misery and anxiety."

The recovery process requires a change in old behavior patterns from the way in which addicted persons live their lives on a daily basis. Ultimately, a goal of recovery is to take the emphasis off the external world, its achievements and material gain, and to look within. Once there, the goal is to heal the inner self. To do this recovering persons must approve, like and love themselves no matter what the external world dictates. Success and outward accomplishments never heal the inner self that has been injured from childhood. Work addicts must reorganize their lives in a way that repositions them and makes them more receptive to the full benefits of recovery. Reorganization of daily routines brings balance to all areas of life and ultimately leads to a spiritual transformation that helps the little unnurtured inner child say, "I'm okay just the way I am."

Seek Spiritual Healing

Many of the problems associated with work addiction can be resolved by reorganizing our lives and practicing certain exercises. A good night's rest, a week by the seashore, a two-mile hike, a healthy meal, a rigorous game of volleyball, fun conversations and interactions with others all can help. But these approaches only scratch the surface. Abusive work habits are not the problems but only the symptoms of deeper seated problems that began in childhood.

Recovery that is limited to mere reduction of work hours with inclusion of recreation and leisure is like putting bandaids on a festering sore. To get to the crux of the addiction, we must look deeper into ourselves. Most work addicts are driven by poor self-esteem. True and lasting recovery can occur only when we address our addiction on a spiritual level. Spirituality is not limited to organized religion but includes a spiritual search through a Higher Power beyond our human selves. Through meditation, prayer, inspirational readings and attendance in a 12-Step program, inner problems are confronted and resolved, and the compulsive need for work balances itself.

It was not until I attended a family treatment program that I was able to put the pieces of my life together. That program, combined with the 12 Steps of Al-Anon, was like looking into a crystal ball. Everything became crystal clear. My understanding the role that being a child of an alcoholic played in who I am helped me begin to grow by leaps and bounds.

Attend A 12-Step Program

There are many groups available to facilitate spiritual growth in recovery. I recommend one of the groups founded on the 12 Steps and Traditions of Alcoholics

Anonymous (AA) and Al-Anon to promote spiritual growth and a new way of life. Al-Anon, Adult Children of Alcoholics groups (ACoAs) and Co-dependents Anonymous (CoDA) all follow the 12 Steps, with chapters across the United States. Addresses of their national headquarters are listed in Chapter 9. They are not aligned with any religion, sect or denomination, nor are they affiliated with any program or organization. They do not accept or receive any financial support aside from voluntary contributions from members.

Al-Anon is a nationwide fellowship of people whose lives have been affected by alcoholism in a family member or close friend. Help is offered by sharing personal experiences, strength and hope, and working through the 12 Steps. The ACoA groups use a 12-Step program of recovery and discovery for adults who were raised in alcoholic homes. The CoDA fellowships are composed of men and women (most of whom came from dysfunctional or alcoholic homes) whose common problem is the inability to maintain functional relationships. The meetings of CoDA are based on the 12 Steps and 12 Traditions of Alcoholics Anonymous. Through a 12-Step program of your choice, daily inspirational readings and a sponsor who will give you support, you will be well equipped in the healing process.

Apply The 12 Steps Of AA

The 12 Steps have worked for millions of people with a variety of addictions, including alcohol and other drugs, food, gambling, shopping and co-dependency. The Steps will also help those who are committed to a program of spiritual recovery from a life of compulsive, uncontrollable and harmful work habits. The steps are vehicles for healing work compulsions and establishing a more meaningful and fulfilled lifestyle.

I have applied the Steps to work addiction. Suggested ways you can apply them in your daily living follow:

Step 1: *We admitted we were powerless over alcohol* **(work)** *— that our lives had become unmanageable.*

The first step is the key to giving up control of abusive work practices. The work abuser admits powerlessness over the ability to manage compulsive work habits. Building on this base, the work abuser admits that compulsive work habits are out of control and uses the support of others who have made similar admissions as a source of strength from continued work abuse practices. The roadblock of know-it-all superiority is removed through the admission of powerlessness and helplessness. Through this admission, human fallibility and humility are acknowledged. This is the basis for admitting you are only human, you cannot do everything by yourself and you are allowed to make mistakes.

Step 2: *Came to believe that a Power greater than ourselves could restore us to sanity.*

As you let go of your control and perfectionism, you start to view your life differently. You realize your attempts to control your addiction only made your life even more unmanageable. This is the beginning of surrender. You realize your way is not *the* way and that only a greater source can restore your sanity. You reinterpret some of your old behavior patterns of overdoing, overcommitting, overcompensating and overcontrolling as sick, even insane. You see that your insatiable drive was mad, crippling and made inhuman demands on yourself and others. Realizing your own human limitations and imperfections awaken the need for help from a Power greater than yourself. As you put your faith in a Higher Power, you will discard these unhealthy behaviors and achieve clarity, soundness of mind and inner peace.

Step 3: *Made a decision to turn our will and our lives over to the care of God* as we understood Him.

Turning your will and life over to the care of a Higher Power means many things. God can be the synergistic help you receive from a group support, a sudden insight you have during an inspirational reading or the realizations received when listening to another group member. The point is that you have surrendered. You have reached for other sources outside yourself for help and support. Your omnipotence is tempered through this simple act, and you stand face to face with others, communicating through a common spirit of humanity. Your ability to interact and enjoy the company of others improves, and that empty void inside starts to fill.

Your willingness to let a Higher Power guide you through your inability to control excessive work habits will also carry over into other areas of your life. You will see that you are powerless over everything and everyone in your life, and that attempting to control other people and situations only creates stress, frustration and further unmanageability. Putting this admission into daily practice on the job, at home and in social settings paradoxically frees workers of addicted patterns, allows them to develop healthy work practices and positively alters their relationships with co-workers, family members and friends. As you turn your work habits and life over to a greater force than yourself, work quality improves and inner knowledge spirals. Worries, concerns and frustrations are resolved through self-insights and inspiration.

Step 4: *Made a searching and fearless moral inventory of ourselves.*

This step helps you identify your weak points and strengthen your strong ones. It helps you realize the traits that are conducive to your growth and the growth of others, as well as those traits that impede growth. For instance, you may identify your inability to delegate work to subordinates or peers, knowing deep inside that many co-workers could perform the task as well as or better than yourself. You may realize that your standards of perfectionism are unrealistic and unfair to those with whom you work, live and play. You will see how intolerance and impatience of those who do not keep the same pace and rigid adherence to your way as opposed to other possible viewpoints, hurt business associates and loved ones.

Essentially, all the disturbing character traits related to your work addiction are unearthed, stare you in the face and compel you to pinpoint behaviors that you want to change. As you take personal stock, you are not putting yourself down or devaluing yourself in any way. You are merely making an objective assessment of the reality of how you thought and behaved when you actively abused work.

Step 5: *Admitted to God, to ourselves and to another human being the exact nature of our wrongs.*

Along the path of life, all of us make mistakes now and then because we are human. Admitting when you are wrong permits you to be human with all its imperfections. Sharing your imperfections with a loved one, a close business associate or a group of recovering adults liberates you from self-flagellation and from the need to justify, rationalize, minimize or attack. We will never be perfect, no matter how hard we try. But we can strive for excellence and try to become the best that we can be. It is important to expect and permit ourselves to make mistakes, and to stop beating ourselves up when we do.

The day will never come when we will not make mistakes. Being able to acknowledge our wrongdoings by saying, "I was wrong; I apologize; but after all, I'm only human," is healing. Permitting ourselves to make mistakes does not mean we become complacent or throw excellence out the window. The goal of self-insight is important only as long as we build in margin for error. When you begin admitting you are wrong, you make giant strides in becoming real, genuine and authentic. As others reciprocate their admissions, you find that your imperfections, wrongdoings and mistakes are shared, and that you are not nearly as bad as you thought you were.

Step 6: *Were entirely ready to have God remove all these defects of character.*

Having recognized and admitted your character defects, you are now ready to let them go. That means giving up all the securities you have clung to since you were a youngster. Actually, it means letting go of that sinking life raft — the need to control, to be perfect and to be on top — that no longer works anyway. It means opening yourself up to a new way of life with all its possibilities of change and having faith that everything will work out better without your control of it. This is a true test of self-security because it means ridding yourself of comfort and complacency, and facing the new and unknown. As you give up your old patterns, new, more healthy and mature ones replace them.

Step 7: *Humbly asked Him to remove our shortcomings.*

Once ready to have character defects removed, this step prepares you to ask for help. At this point, you ask for the imperfections, which you have acknowledged, to be removed. Making a *humble plea*, rather than a *strong demand*, goes against the grain of the addicted worker's temperament and presents a true challenge to the abuser's humility.

As old shortcomings evaporate, you will begin a metamorphosis of who you are. Work associates, family and friends will marvel at the change in "the new you." They, in turn, will begin to respond to you in new and more approving ways. You will attract new and interesting people in your life through social and business contacts. The quality of work improves along with your ability to interact with others on an equal basis. Your old relationships will undergo change. Some of them will become more intense and close-knit. You will discard others because, for the first time, you can see them for the dysfunctional relationships that they are.

Step 8: *Made a list of all persons we had harmed, and became willing to make amends to them all.*

This step takes you on a life review of sorts and actually suggests that you write down all the family, friends and colleagues you have harmed by your abusive work habits. Perhaps you'll list a time you jumped down the secretary's throat for forgetting to mail an important letter; a time you worked late and missed your daughter's first piano recital; or the many times you scolded a loved one, who in begging for a portion of your attention, interrupted your train of thought.

Addictive work habits cause neglect of family, insensitivity to the needs of others, suppression of love from those you really care about, rejection of anyone who cannot meet your high standards, or belittlement of those who do not conduct business or bake bread as fast or in the exact way as you. You accept your past self-righteous behaviors, without guilt, and commit yourself to changing them. As you make your list, you forgive yourself as well as promise to make amends to everyone who was hurt in the aftermath of your work addiction.

Step 9: *Made direct amends to such people wherever possible, except when to do so would injure them or others.*

The mistakes of the past can never be totally erased, but they can be mended. From all the people you have hurt through your addiction, now is the time to ask their forgiveness. One of the best ways to mend past injuries is to change old behaviors. The moment you tell family and co-workers that you are in recovery from work addiction, the process of making direct amends has begun.

Making amends must be done without guilt or obligation, and out of desire and commitment. You spend more quality time with your family because you enjoy it; you are patient and courteous to the super-market cashier whom you ridiculed and maligned for being "too slow" because she is doing the best she can; you recognize and compliment co-workers for a job well done because they deserve it; you advise employees to slow down and take it easy because you care about them; you pay attention to your own personal needs because you are worth the attention; you apologize to colleagues for pushing them too hard because you regret it or you help your family with household chores because it is your responsibility to do your part.

During the amendment process, you will suddenly realize that the little child inside of you has grown up and that you are a more mature and responsible adult. You have restored your self-respect and the respect of others.

Step 10: *Continued to take personal inventory and when we were wrong promptly admitted it.*

Maintain a climate of honesty and openness at the factory, at the office and at home. Get in the habit of continued self-examination, admitting mistakes and imperfections, and allowing others to make mistakes too. Learn to forgive yourself and others, establishing work schedules and deadlines that are reasonable, and that reduce stress and improve productivity. You understand that no one ever arrives at perfection, and that life is a series of lessons and mistakes from which to learn. Self-maintenance is a continual life-long process of self-examination and self-insights that keeps all of us on track.

Step 11: *Sought through prayer and meditation to improve our conscious contact with God* as we understood Him, *praying only for knowledge of His will for us and the power to carry that out.*

Your spiritual development becomes just as integral as work and family. And you include it in your daily life. Developing spirituality can be accomplished in an assortment of ways such as organized religion. Spiritual life is also built around such themes as the golden rule, meditation, world peace, environmental harmony and a committed value system. Finding and living a spiritual life nurtures your inner needs. Going with the flow of what truly feels right inside leads you to avenues of life that yield excitement, adventure and fulfillment. Your spiritual awakening makes you feel centered, grounded and self-confident. Self-affirmations replace seeking approval from others.

Through self-examination, meditation and prayer you become connected with the past, present and future through a Higher "Knowing" — one that knows who you are, where you are and where you are headed. And you allow that Higher Power to guide you in the right direction.

Step 12: *Having had a spiritual awakening as the result of these steps, we tried to carry this message to alcoholics* **(work addicts)** *and to practice these principles in all our affairs.*

This step is a culmination of the others as you return what you have received back to the universe. You give freely of yourself not out of obligation but out of love. You may get involved with an employee assistance program at work, start a rap group to prevent burnout on the job, take a new employee under your wing or become someone's sponsor who suffers from work addiction, or you may live your life by example.

Putting all the principles into practice helps you connect from the heart, instead of from just the head. Relationships become healthier, and positive people come into your life. You will radiate and attract people through your deeds and actions, and become a positive role model for others. Many nonrecovering friends or co-workers might want to know how they can also have whatever you have discovered. You will have opportunities to share (without preaching, lecturing or advising) your spiritual growth with those who want to know. The best forum for such sharing is in a 12-Step program where people assemble willingly out of a committed desire to change.

As you share your message with others, you touch and help them transform their lives as you did yours. You will be spiritually strengthened by their message as well. The cycle perpetuates itself. As you share your spiritual awakening, you send out positive energy that helps others transform their lives; this, in turn, comes back to enrich your own life a thousand-fold.

The Power Of Choice

We are all creators of our own destinies, puppeteers of our own strings. It's up to each and every one of us to create what we want in our lives. For those of us who are addicted to work, there is hope. But it is up to us to make it happen. Memories and problems of the past can never be fully erased, but their effects on us can be rerouted. The one thing no one can take away from us is the power of choice. We can choose to view ourselves as victims of dysfunctional upbringings and continue to live with the misery of addiction. Or we can choose to interpret our hard, early lives as lessons that have taught us to live with quality. No matter how horrendous our yesterdays, if we choose to, we can transform them into happy and fulfilling todays and tomorrows. The choice is ours.

The Road To Recovery

I used to ask, "Who is he?"
As I tried to find the real me.
I seemed fairly nice, but I never could tell.
I was not able to know myself well.
I did not know me, but I guess I should,
Try and get acquainted if I could.
Work had been my whole life, you see.
So I knew nothing about the Road to Recovery.
I knew I would have to look deeper inside,
Where all my emotions and thoughts reside.
I didn't want to keep those things to myself,
All locked in a closet on a neat little shelf.
I wanted to open that door and say,
Come on out of there, now; it's okay.
I dreaded the thoughts of living eternally,
Without the Road to Recovery.

I tore down the dark walls of 40-odd years,
And set free the anger, the hurt and the fears.
I transformed those addictive feelings of mine,
Into patience, love, joy and sunshine.
I removed the KEEP OUT sign that set me free,
Of all the Roadblocks to Recovery.

In my strenuous strivings all I had left,
Was a fantastic feeling, an awareness of self.
Through the 12 Steps I made amends,
And asked for forgiveness from my loved ones and friends.
I looked into my soul and around inside,
And left my shell where I had tried to hide.
With arms outstretched I made a decree,
"From this day forth I'm on the Road to Recovery!"

With love,
Bryan Robinson

References And
Further Readings

This chapter contains references for further reading on the subject of work addiction, co-dependence and children of alcoholics. I have included a list of annotations of books, names of organizations, periodicals and other resources.

Books

I have organized the readings in the following list by their thematic emphasis into one of the following categories: Children of Alcoholics, Co-dependence, Healing and Breaking the Cycle, Work Addiction, and Stress.

Children of Alcoholics

Black, Claudia. **It Will Never Happen To Me.** Denver, CO: M.A.C. Publications, 1982. This shares some of the experiences of children of alcoholics and explains the process of how children develop their roles of super-responsible, placating, adjusting and acting-out children.

Cermak, Timmen. **A Primer On Adult Children Of Alcoholics.** Deerfield Beach, FL: Health Communications, 1989. About adult children of alcoholics, this book identifies issues and steps to recovery.

Gravitz, Herbert, and Bowden, Julie. **Guide To Recovery: A Book For Adult Children Of Alcoholics.** Holmes Beach, FL: Learning Publications, 1985. Answers to more than 75 questions typically asked by adult children of alcoholics are given, as well as a description of the stages of recovery from the effects of parental alcoholism.

Kritsberg, Wayne. **The ACoA Syndrome: From Discovery To Recovery.** Pompano Beach, FL: Health Communications, 1985. The foundations for healing the wounds of an alcoholic-influenced childhood are laid in this book. The author identifies four family types through which co-dependence is transmitted from one generation to the next.

Robinson, Bryan. **Working With Children Of Alcoholics: The Practitioner's Handbook.** Lexington, MA: Lexington Books, 1989. A comprehensive guide for practitioners in all helping professions, this shows, through clinical experience and case studies, the problems children of alcoholics have, their identification and their treatment.

Seixas, Judith, and Youcha, Geraldine. **Children Of Alcoholism: A Survivor's Manual.** New York: Crown Publishers, 1985. This shows what happened in childhood to make adult children as they are, and also presents ideas on what to do about dysfunctional behaviors.

Somers, Suzanne. **Keeping Secrets.** New York: Warner Books, 1988. An autobiographical and candid account, the author shows how alcoholism robbed this celebrity of her childhood. It reminded me a lot of my own childhood.

Woititz, Janet. **Adult Children Of Alcoholics.** Pompano Beach, FL: Health Communications, 1983. This best-selling book is an excellent overview to the personality traits of adult children. It presents insights on how upbringing in chemically dependent families can be carried into adulthood and what can be done to change these patterns.

Co-dependence

Beattie, Melody. **Co-dependent No More.** Center City, MO: Hazelden, 1987. One of the best books out on co-dependence, the author shows in a very clear style what it is and what you can do about it.

Bradshaw, John. **Bradshaw On: The Family: A Revolutionary Way Of Self-Discovery.** Pompano Beach, FL: Health Communications, 1988. The author guides the reader out of dysfunction and proposes how problems within the family can be remedied.

Friel, John, and Friel, Linda. **Adult Children: The Secret Of Dysfunctional Families.** Pompano Beach, FL: Health Communications, 1988. Defining the problems of dysfunctional families and analyzing the characteristic symptoms, this offers guidelines to live healthy, happy lives now.

Smith, Ann. **Grandchildren Of Alcoholics: Another Generation Of Co-dependency.** Pompano Beach, FL: Health Communications, 1988. This pinpoints the problems of those living in families where a grandparent is or was an alcoholic, and where the parents are therefore children of alcoholics with the resulting dysfunctional parenting skills.

Subby, Robert. **Lost In The Shuffle: The Co-dependent Reality.** Pompano Beach, FL: Health Communications, 1987. This is written for those who seek to understand the condition of co-dependency, the problems, the pitfalls, the unreal rules the co-dependent lives by and the way out of the diseased condition to recovery.

Wegscheider, Sharon. **Another Chance: Hope And Health For The Alcoholic Family.** Palo Alto, CA: Science & Behavior Books, 1980. The author integrates family therapy and alcoholism, and explains and exposes the feelings and frustrations of family members living with an alcoholic.

Wegscheider-Cruse, Sharon. **Choicemaking.** Pompano Beach, FL: Health Communications, 1985. For those recovering from co-dependency, the author integrates her personal experiences as a child of alcoholic parents with professional knowledge to foster spiritual transformation.

Healing And Breaking The Cycle

Lerner, Rokelle. **Daily Affirmations For Adult Children Of Alcoholics.** Pompano Beach, FL: Health Communications, 1985. These affirmations provide a daily source of inspiration to change the distorted and undermining messages of childhood in an alcoholic family.

Middelton-Moz, Jane, and Dwinell, Lorie. **After The Tears: Reclaiming The Personal Losses Of Childhood.** Pompano Beach, FL: Health Communications, 1986. Children raised in an alcoholic environment will perpetuate the alcoholic legacy even if they never drink. This book shows readers how to mourn the loss of childhood and recapture their self-worth.

O'Gorman, Patricia, and Oliver-Diaz, Philip. **Breaking The Cycle Of Addiction: A Parent's Guide To Raising Healthy Kids.** Pompano Beach, FL: Health Communications, 1987. Especially for parents or prospective parents who were raised in addicted or dysfunctional families, this book helps break the compulsion that is frequently passed on through family dynamics.

Whitfield, Charles. **Healing The Child Within: Discovery And Recovery For Adult Children Of Dysfunc-**

tional Families. Pompano Beach, FL: Health Communications, 1987. This defines, describes and discovers how we can find our child within. It shows how we can gently heal and nurture this child until we can reach the role of spirituality within it, and how we can live the free life we were meant to live.

Woititz, Janet. **Struggle For Intimacy.** Pompano Beach, FL: Health Communications, 1985. The author reveals the barriers to trust and the intimacy learned early in life by children of alcoholics. Tips for rebuilding intimacy in adult relationships are provided.

Work Addiction

Rohrlich, Jay. **Work And Love: The Crucial Balance.** New York: Summit Books, 1980. Distinguishing between devotion to work and addiction to work, the author suggests ways to balance work and love.

Schaef, Anne, and Fassel, Diane. **Addictive Organizations.** San Francisco: Harper & Row, 1988. The authors show how many organizations are affected by addictions and what the addictive world view is. These groups themselves even function exactly like an active individual addict. Many behaviors considered "normal" for workers and reinforced in the workplace are actually those of an active addict or a nonrecovering co-dependent.

Schaef, Anne. **When Society Becomes An Addict.** San Francisco: Harper & Row, 1987. Anne Schaef suggests that addictive behavior is now the norm in society, which has begun to function as an active addict itself.

Sprankle, Judith, and Ebel, Henry. **The Workaholic Syndrome: Your Job Is Not Your Life!** New York: Walker & Company, 1987. The authors, both communications consultants, discuss workaholism as a social trend in which most Americans use their jobs

— rather than their personal and family lives — to define their identities. Workaholism is discussed as the new American work ethic that can be reversed instead of a disease, like work addiction, that requires a deeper analysis and commitment to change.

Woititz, Janet. **Home Away From Home: The Art Of Self-Sabotage.** Pompano Beach, FL: Health Communications, 1987. This gives answers to such questions as: What are the best jobs for ACoAs? Do all ACoAs end up as workaholics? How can they prevent burnout?

Woodside, Migs. **Children Of Alcoholics On The Job.** New York: Children of Alcoholics Foundation, 1986. The first publication for corporations and Employee Assistance Programs about children of alcoholics in the workplace, its message offers hope and concrete, practical suggestions to reduce corporate health care and other costs, and to prevent pain and unhappiness experienced by millions of adult children.

Stress

Braiker, Harriet. **The Type E Woman.** New York: Signet, 1986. For women who feel they must be as good as any man in the workplace and as good as any woman at home, the author identifies Type E behaviors as those in women who carry this double burden and feel they must be everything to everybody.

Brenner, Avis. **Helping Children Cope With Stress.** Lexington, MA: Lexington Books, 1984. The author presents tips on how to relieve stress in children's lives so that they can grow and develop in healthier ways.

Davis, Martha, Eshelman, Elizabeth, and McKay, Matthew. **The Relaxation And Stress Reduction Workbook.** Oakland, CA: New Harbinger Publications, 1982. A wonderful book of exercises with step-by-step directions on reducing stress, this includes progressive relaxation, self-hypnosis, meditation, autogenics, imagination, nutrition, biofeedback, assertiveness training, breathing, time management, exercise and thought stopping.

Cooper, Cary. **The Stress Check: Coping With The Stresses Of Life And Work.** Englewood Cliffs, NJ: Prentice-Hall, 1981. This is one of the best resources to learn about the sources of stress at work, and to reduce that stress through helpful hints and stress-reduction exercises.

Elkind, David. **The Hurried Child.** Reading, MA: Addison-Wesley, 1981. Describing children under stress and society's pushing children to grow up before they are developmentally ready, this offers insights, advice and hope for solving these problems.

Friedman, Meyer, and Rosenman, Ray. **Type A Behavior And Your Heart.** New York: Knopf, 1974. Reporting the results of a longitudinal study of 3,000 healthy, middle-aged men, this book distinguishes Type A from Type B behaviors and shows the association between Type A personality, heart and other physical ailments.

Saunders, Antoinette, and Remsberg, Bonnie. **The Stress-Proof Child: A Loving Parent's Guide.** New York: Holt, Rinehart & Winston, 1985. The book explores many ways parents can remove stress in their children's lives.

Witkin-Lanoil, Georgia. **The Female Stress Syndrome.** New York: Berkley Publishing, 1984. This identifies the stresses and stress symptoms that are uniquely or more frequently experienced by females.

Witkin-Lanoil, Georgia. **The Male Stress Syndrome.** New York: Berkley Publishing, 1986. The author explores why men develop certain stresses, what those physical and psychological stresses are to which men are particularly susceptible and what they can do about it.

Wuertzer, Patricia, and May, Lucinda. **Relax, Recover: Stress Management For Recovering People.** Center City, MO: Hazelden, 1988. Helping you to evaluate the role that stress plays in your life, the authors describe a stress management program that includes support, exercise, meditation, relaxation techniques and biofeedback.

Organizations

This section lists the major organizations concerned with adult children of alcoholics issues, family co-dependence and work addiction.

Adult Children of Alcoholics Central Service Board, P.O. Box 3216, 2522 West Sepulveda Blvd., Suite 200, Torrance, CA 90505. A 12-Step suggested program of recovery/discovery is for adults who were raised in alcoholic homes. The office serves as a clearinghouse for information to, from and about the growing fellowship of adult children of alcoholics around the world.

Alcoholics Anonymous, P.O. Box 459, Grand Central Station, New York, NY 10163. This is a fellowship of men and women who share their experience, strength and hope with each other so that they may solve their common problem and help others recover from alcoholism. The only requirement for membership is a desire to stop drinking.

Al-Anon/Alateen Family Group Headquarters, P.O. Box 182, Madison Square Station, New York, NY 10159. Through this nationwide fellowship of young people, usually teenagers, whose lives have been affected by alcoholism in a family member or close friend, help is offered by sharing of personal experiences, strength and hope.

Children of Alcoholics Foundation, Inc., 31st Floor, 200 Park Avenue, New York, NY 10166. A nonprofit, public organization created to assist this country's 28 million children of alcoholic parents, the Foundation has the primary goals of raising awareness of the intergenerational links in the disease of alcoholism, helping reduce the suffering and pain by those from alcoholic homes and preventing future alcoholism.

Co-dependents Anonymous, National Service Office, P.O. Box 5508, Glendale, AZ 85312. Co-dependents Anonymous is a fellowship of men and women whose common problem is an inability to maintain functional relationships. CoDA bases its meetings on AA's 12 Steps and 12 Traditions. Its meetings are open to those who feel they are in a co-dependent relationship and feel overly responsible for others' feelings and behaviors.

Families Anonymous, P.O. Box 528, Van Nuys, CA 91408. This organization is for relatives and friends concerned about the use of drugs or related behavioral problems. It uses the 12 Steps of Alcoholics Anonymous to help families recover.

National Association for Children of Alcoholics, 31582 Coast Highway, Suite B, South Laguna, CA 92677. A national nonprofit organization, this was founded in 1983 to support and serve as a resource for children of alcoholics of all ages and for those in a position to help them. NACoA believes that children of alcoholics deserve the understanding, information and help they need to break out of their isolation and silence.

National Council on Alcoholism, Inc., 12 West 21st Street, New York, NY 10010. This is a national nonprofit organization combating alcoholism, other drug addictions and related problems. Major programs include prevention and education, public information, public policy advocacy, medical/scientific information, conferences and publications.

Periodicals

This section highlights important periodicals in the field that publish articles pertaining to addiction, co-dependence, family dysfunction and work addiction. I have organized the periodicals by newsletters published by organizations to keep readers and members up-to-date, and magazines written for the popular market and professionals in the field of addictions.

Newsletters

The Addiction Newsletter. Published monthly, this newsletter serves as a resource exchange for professionals in preventing and treating alcoholism and drug abuse. *Manisses Communications Group, Inc., P.O. Box 3357, Wayland Square, Providence, RI 02906.*

CoA Review. An international newsletter, this is for those concerned about children of alcoholics. *Thomas Perrin, Inc., P.O. Box 423, Rutherford, NJ 07070.*

Grapevine. This international monthly journal of Alcoholics Anonymous presents the experiences and opinions of AA members and others interested in AA's recovery program. *AA, P.O. Box 459, Grand Central Station, New York, NY 10163.*

Our Voice. This is a newsletter about chemical dependency and treatment in the gay and lesbian community. *The Pride Institute, 14400 Martin Drive, Eden Prairie, MN 55344.*

NACoA Network. A quarterly newsletter for the National Association for Children of Alcoholics, it announces the latest in national movements, research, conferences and other national news. *NACoA, 31582 Coast Highway, Suite B, South Laguna, CA 92677.*

Magazines

Alcoholism: The National Magazine. Published bimonthly by Alcom, Inc., this magazine is for recovered alcoholics, professionals in the field, and family and friends of still-drinking alcoholics. *The Editor, Alcoholism Magazine, Box C19051, Seattle, WA 98109.*

Alcoholism And Addiction Magazine. Published bimonthly, the magazine presents information on all the addictions, including work, food, sex and substances. It is written in a readable style for the lay person as well as the practitioner. *P.O. Box 31329, Seattle, WA 98103.*

Changes. This magazine is devoted strictly for and about adult children issues and is published six times a year. *The U.S. Journal, Inc., 3201 S.W. 15th Street, Deerfield Beach, FL 33442.*

Focus On Chemically Dependent Families. This is the first magazine to devote its entire contents to the effects of chemical dependency on families and children. It has a special column in each issue on co-dependency. *The U.S. Journal, Inc., 3201 S.W. 15th Street, Deerfield Beach, FL 33442.*

The Forum. This international monthly journal of Al-Anon is a publication for, about and written by family members who have been affected by alcoholism. *Al-Anon Family Group Headquarters, Inc., 1372 Broadway, New York, NY 10018.*

Other Books By . . .

HEALTH COMMUNICATIONS, INC.

Enterprise Center
3201 Southwest 15th Street
Deerfield Beach, FL 33442
Phone: 800-851-9100

ADULT CHILDREN OF ALCOHOLICS
Janet Woititz
Over a year on The New York Times Best Seller list,this book is the primer
on Adult Children of Alcoholics.
ISBN 0-932194-15-X   **$6.95**

STRUGGLE FOR INTIMACY
Janet Woititz
Another best seller, this book gives insightful advice on learning to love
more fully.
ISBN 0-932194-25-7   **$6.95**

DAILY AFFIRMATIONS: For Adult Children of Alcoholics
Rokelle Lerner
These positive affirmations for every day of the year paint a mental picture
of your life as you choose it to be.
ISBN 0-932194-27-3   **$6.95**

*CHOICEMAKING: For Co-dependents, Adult Children and Spirituality
Seekers* — Sharon Wegscheider-Cruse
This useful book defines the problems and solves them in a positive way.
ISBN 0-932194-26-5   **$9.95**

LEARNING TO LOVE YOURSELF: Finding Your Self-Worth
Sharon Wegscheider-Cruse
"Self-worth is a choice, not a birthright", says the author as she shows us
how we can choose positive self-esteem.
ISBN 0-932194-39-7   **$7.95**

LET GO AND GROW: Recovery for Adult Children
Robert Ackerman
An in-depth study of the different characteristics of adult children of
alcoholics with guidelines for recovery.
ISBN 0-932194-51-6   **$8.95**

LOST IN THE SHUFFLE: The Co-dependent Reality
Robert Subby
A look at the unreal rules the co-dependent lives by and the way out of the
dis-eased reality.
ISBN 0-932194-45-1   **$8.95**

New Books . . .
from Health Communications

BRADSHAW ON: THE FAMILY: A Revolutionary Way of Self-Discovery
John Bradshaw
The host of the nationally televised series of the same name shows us how families can be healed and we as individuals can realize our full potential.
ISBN 0-932194-54-0 **$9.95**

HEALING THE CHILD WITHIN: Discovery and recovery for Adult Children of Dysfunctional Families — Charles Whitfield
Dr. Whitfield defines, describes and discovers how we can reach our Child Within to heal and nurture our woundedness.
ISBN 0-932194-40-0 **$8.95**

WHISKY'S SONG: An Explicit Story of Surviving in an Alcoholic Home
Mitzi Chandler
A beautiful but brutal story of growing up where violence and neglect are everyday occurrences conveys a positive message of survival and love.
ISBN 0-932194-42-7 **$6.95**

New Books on Spiritual Recovery . . .
from Health Communications

THE JOURNEY WITHIN: A Spiritual Path to Recovery
Ruth Fishel
This book will lead you from your dysfunctional beginnings to the place within where renewal occurs.
ISBN 0-932194-41-9 **$8.95**

LEARNING TO LIVE IN THE NOW: 6-Week Personal Plan To Recovery
Ruth Fishel
The author gently introduces you to the valuable healing tools of meditation, positive creative visualization and affirmations.
ISBN 0-932194-62-1 **$7.95**

GENESIS: Spirituality in Recovery for Co-dependents
by Julie D. Bowden and Herbert L. Gravitz
A self-help spiritual program for adult children of trauma, an in-depth look at "turning it over" and "letting go".
ISBN 0-932194-56-7 **$6.95**

GIFTS FOR PERSONAL GROWTH AND RECOVERY
Wayne Kritsberg
Gifts for healing which include journal writing, breathing, positioning and meditation.
ISBN 0-932194-60-5 **$6.95**

Books from . . .
Health Communications

THIRTY-TWO ELEPHANT REMINDERS: A Book of Healthy Rules
Mary M. McKee
Concise advice by 32 wise elephants whose wit and good humor will also
be appearing in a 12-step calendar and greeting cards.
ISBN 0-932194-59-1 $3.95

BREAKING THE CYCLE OF ADDICTION: For Adult Children of Alcoholics
Patricia O'Gorman and Philip Oliver-Diaz
For parents who were raised in addicted families, this guide teaches you
about Breaking the Cycle of Addiction from *your* parents to your children.
Must reading for any parent.
ISBN 0-932194-37-0 $8.95

AFTER THE TEARS: Reclaiming The Personal Losses of Childhood
Jane Middelton-Moz and Lorie Dwinnel
Your lost childhood must be grieved in order for you to recapture your
self-worth and enjoyment of life. This book will show you how.
ISBN 0-932194-36-2 $7.95

ADULT CHILDREN OF ALCOHOLICS SYNDROME: From Discovery to Recovery
Wayne Kritsberg
Through the Family Integration System and foundations for healing the
wounds of an alcoholic-influenced childhood are laid in this important
book.
ISBN 0-932194-30-3 $7.95

OTHERWISE PERFECT: People and Their Problems with Weight
Mary S. Stuart and Lynnzy Orr
This book deals with all the varieties of eating disorders, from anorexia to
obesity, and how to cope sensibly and successfully.
ISBN 0-932194-57-5 $7.95

Orders must be prepaid by check, money order, MasterCard or Visa.
Purchase orders from agencies accepted (attach P.O. documentation)
for billing. Net 30 days.

Minimum shipping/handling — $1.25 for orders less than $25. For
orders over $25, add 5% of total for shipping and handling. Florida
residents add 5% sales tax.